Loving Someone with an Eating Disorder

How to Survive and Come Out Together

Biella Blom

Loving Someone with an Eating Disorder

ISBN: 9781696934121

Warning and Disclaimer

Publisher contact

Skinny Bottle Publishing

books@skinnybottle.com

BIELLA BLOM

Introduction

Eating disorders are not a lifestyle choice!

They are a serious mental illness that comes with physical complications that can lead to death. The fragile and complicated dynamics of eating disorders are not well understood, and myths abound. Suffers don't know how to control their condition, or how to get help. And people who love them become worn down and desperate as they watch their loved ones slowly and systematically kill themselves.

This book is for people who love someone that has an eating disorder. It is for those who stand helplessly witnessing another's life of subtle obsession, denial, anxiety, depression, physical illness, and impending death unless they can change their way. It is for those who themselves have become desperate, who can see no light at the end of the tunnel, and who are frantically searching for hope.

You can find online resources and books that delve into the theory of eating disorders, as well as publications that offer excellent psychoanalysis of eating disorders. But this book is none of those. It's intended as a practical guide for people who love someone that is suffering from an eating disorder.

When you are desperate and losing hope, you are not looking for insight into your fears from an academic. You want honest, practical, everyday insight to help you understand the situation. Above all, you are looking for direction and hope. You want to know if the situation can be turned around. Is there recovery and healing?

This book will offer you hope, but will also expose the reality of eating disorders and shed light on how they take hold in the mind of the sufferer. I offer no hard and fast solutions because with mental illness there aren't any. Recovery from mental illness depends on the sufferer and the environment the sufferer finds themselves in, be it by choice or an imposed environment. You must accept that as a witness, recovery is never in your control. But your love and your constant, non-judgemental presence can be the strength the sufferer needs to guide them through the dark days of early recovery and back into the light.

I have not included any statistics in this book because statistics vary extensively from one organization to another and from one country to another. I believe this is because of the ignorance around eating disorders and the stigma attached to mental illness. Many people will not admit to having an eating disorder, or that a loved one has an eating disorder out of fear of stigmatization and social rejection.

The prime difference between mental illness and physical illness is that mental illness carries a stigma, and often people who are diagnosed with mental illness are rejected or ridiculed, even by family and people in their inner circle. The stigma can be so intense that it can prevent the sufferer from finding employment, and can cost friendships, relationships, and other opportunities. On the contrary, physical illness garners sympathy, support and often unites families.

No one is immune from mental illness and therefore eating disorders, just as no one is immune from physical illness and disease. There is no gender, race, age, culture or socio-economic group that is more or less susceptible to eating disorders. Once you accept that eating disorders are a mental illness that can affect anyone, this concept will sit more comfortably.

But the fear of stigma can cause families to deny mental illness, and also push the sufferer into denial. Some people accept the diagnosis of an eating disorder, but they refuse to accept that it is a symptom of mental illness. Whether it is the attitude of the sufferer or their loved ones, fear of stigma will always impede recovery. To recover, you have to understand the underlying problems and accept them; only if you accept them can you properly address them to find healing and recovery. Any reservation or denial from the sufferer and their loved ones will prevent the underlying causes from being addressed.

Just like physical illness can be treated and the person can make a full recovery, so too mental illness can be treated, and the person can make a full recovery. Eating disorders are a pattern of wrongful thinking. Wrongful thinking could be self-taught or learned from other people. Whichever way, with acceptance, focus, support, and dedication whatever has been taught can be untaught and whatever has been learned can be unlearned. We can overwrite our thought patterns.

When I was in my mid-teens, I unwittingly developed anorexia nervosa. At the time I hadn't heard of anorexia nervosa, and I didn't know anything about eating disorders. I had also never been concerned about my weight because I had been a thin child that developed into a thin teen. By my late teens, I had developed bulimia nervosa in tandem with anorexia nervosa. I knew that I was controlling my weight in an unhealthy way, and I knew instinctively to keep it secret, but I had no understanding of the problem, or of the severe consequences these behaviors cause. Anorexia nervosa and bulimia nervosa were to stay with me for another twenty years. The intensity of the condition would fluctuate depending on my life circumstances, but the condition never abated completely. There were times when my weight would drop so low that I could not sit on a firm surface, or in a bath without feeling pain; my body had absolutely no padding. And then there were times when I would gain weight, but I have never been overweight. I developed health problems, and my immune system was compromised. As a result, I constantly developed respiratory infections and regularly coped with a low-grade fever. Going to see a doctor was not an option in case I was asked too many questions, so I just lived with constant illness. I also felt faint very often and fainted quite regularly. But nothing stopped me. I had an excuse for everything; I lived in denial.

I have been in recovery for almost a decade. I wanted to recover, and I found recovery, but I would never have survived early recovery if it was not for the love and support that surrounded me. I want to give you some insight into the distorted and irrational thinking of a sufferer and expose the fear, desperation, and powerlessness of living with an eating disorder. This book will expose the myths, offer you facts and truths, help you to see the light and guide you towards acceptance and hopefully your loved one's recovery.

Creative Insight

I hope that this poem will give you some insight into this
mind of someone suffering from an eating disorder:

Distortions in the mirror

Twisted thoughts

Mind confused

Am I the grotesque?

The fleeting muse?

Pain to pleasure

The source denied

Truth to fiction

Reality defied.

World beyond reach

Faces look the same

A stranger in my skin

Sharing the same name.

Stranger and I are one

I search for that space

From within I look out

I deny my own face.

Chapter 1

What are Eating Disorders?

Eating disorders are broadly defined as "a mental illness that causes serious disturbances in a person's everyday diet. It can manifest as eating extremely small amounts of food or severely overeating. Obsession with eating food takes over a person's life, leading to severe changes in lifestyle and health."

Behind that definition lies extensive and extremely complicated mental catalysts, triggers, thought patterns and deceptions. Eating disorders almost always coexist with other mental illnesses like depression, substance abuse or anxiety disorders.

Although eating disorders are now correctly defined as a mental illness, they very quickly cause physical illness. The longer the sufferer perpetuates the self-destructive behavior patterns, the more severe the physical

14

consequences. Physiological damage can lead to permanent organ failure and death. Eating disorders also come with a high suicide rate.

Although we will discuss common myths later on in the book, I would like to dispel one of the most common myths early on. It goes something like this:

"Eating disorders are a lifestyle choice motivated by vanity."

Nothing could be further from the truth. Although bodyweight does become an obsession with everyone caught in the grips of an eating disorder, it has very little, if anything to do with vanity. Most people who get caught up in obsessive, self-destructive behaviors have three things in common:

1.   Anxiety

2.   Low self-esteem

3.   Poor coping skills

Neither of those three points comfortably pair themselves with vanity. If vanity has any place in eating disorders, it is the concept fuelled by a society that champions perfection and winning at all costs. A person with low self-esteem does not believe that they can live up to society's standards, so they may try harder to gain outside approval, but that is a vulnerability, not vanity. To better understand the banality of this myth, consider uncontrolled overeating, or binge eating, which is as much an eating disorder like anorexia nervosa and bulimia nervosa. Few people would consider a morbidly obese person to be overeating out of vanity. Most people would readily accept that a morbidly obese person probably has a negative self-image. All people with eating disorders have a negative self-image!

Anorexia Nervosa

The earliest documented descriptions of anorexia nervosa are by an English physician, Richard Morton in 1689. But the medical profession didn't recognize anorexia nervosa as a medical condition until the late 19th century. In 1873 a personal physician of Queen Victoria, Sir William Gull, published a seminal paper detailing case descriptions and treatments of anorexia nervosa. French physician, Ernest-Charles Lasègue, also published a paper detailing similar cases in the same year.

Anorexia nervosa was then widely recognized as a medical condition, but knowledge was reserved for the medical profession only until 1978 when a work by German-American psychoanalyst Hilde Bruch brought it to the attention of the broader public. Following the publication, the 1983 death of Karen Carpenter of the popular duo The Carpenters thrust anorexia nervosa into mainstream media.

Anorexia nervosa is characterized by a driving fear of, or determination not to, gain weight. It's not worth splitting hairs here to theorize over the difference between fear and determination because both yield the same result: severely controlled food intake, and a daily pattern of eating substantially less than is necessary to maintain a healthy weight and lead an active lifestyle. Some sufferers restrict and control their food intake to feel in control of their body weight. This is mostly because there are areas of their life that they believe they cannot control. Having control over their body weight, no matter how distorted their impressions, gives them a sense of power over a life that is dominated by powerlessness (genuine or perceived). For other sufferers, restricting and controlling their food intake and body weight is a means of expressing emotions that they are unable to face such as emotional pain and anxiety. Many of these people treat the physical pain caused by extreme hunger as an outlet from a self-harm perspective, much the same as people who resort to cutting. In other words, the pain of self-harm is a valid outlet for the emotional pain that the sufferer cannot, or refuses to face.

I understand that to a healthy mind this kind of thinking must seem otherworldly, but to the anorexic, it is a daily reality. This type of thinking is mostly kept away from other people, and few anorexics will verbalize it. If you do get wind of these thoughts don't challenge them; not even lovingly! Saying things like "but why would you think that" or "what's wrong with you?" will push the anorexic away and deeper into the secrecy of their disease. Remember, an anorexic is not thinking rationally, and their sense of reality has become warped. If you cannot comprehend and find anything supportive to say, rather say nothing. Later, if the anorexic goes into treatment, you can speak more openly. While caught up in the dark vortex of eating disorders, all sufferers are lost, emotionally fragile and very vulnerable.

Each anorexia nervosa sufferer will have their unique reasons for progressing into the disease. There is believed to be a genetic predisposition, and environmental and social factors can weigh in strongly as well. It can be triggered by dieting and exercise to meet society's norms, but for dieting and weight loss to become a destructive obsession, there has to be a pre-existing mental and emotional vulnerability that leads to low self-esteem. Confidence and self-esteem are not the same things. You can be outwardly confident while simultaneously harboring severe unspoken doubts about yourself, leading to low self-esteem.

Anorexia nervosa that is brought on by dieting and exercise to meet society's norms proliferates in both sexes. In girls and women, it can be to meet society's norms of the perfect slim figure, while boys and men aim to meet the taut, muscular frame that society dictates. Both sexes are also prone to anorexia nervosa if they are actively involved in sport, and staying in peak condition is vital to their success. Many people can diet and exercise within the means of what their bodies can take. They stay healthy and know when enough is enough. So dieting and exercise are not the cause of anorexia nervosa, the person's mental state is.

All anorexia nervosa sufferers have a distorted self-image. They have a mental fixation with their body that does not correlate realistically with the facts. They also deny the negative physiological symptoms of their obsessive behavior. Their obsession with controlling weight loss is to the exclusion of any realistic acknowledgment that their actions are causing physical illness. All focus and

18

attention is diverted from physical health and wellbeing and plowed into their obsession with losing and keeping weight off.

Most anorexia nervosa sufferers go to great lengths to study nutrition and in particular calories or kilojoules. Some have a calorie or kilojoule counter with them wherever they go, and others learn calories and kilojoules by heart and only stick to foods that feel safe. The amount of food taken in at any meal is always limited and controlled, either at mealtime or immediately afterward.

There are two main types of anorexia nervosa termed Restricting Subtype and Binge Eating/Purging Subtype. I am going to combine both types so that this book does not become complicated. Briefly explained, sufferers of the Restricting Subtype severely restrict their food intake, controlling the amount and type of food they eat. Sufferers of the Binge Eating/Purging Subtype also control the amount and type of food they eat but can fall into binge eating on occasion. If they do lapse into binge eating, they immediately afterward become consumed by guilt and disgust at their loss of self-control. Binge eating is followed closely by attempts to rid their body of what they have eaten by self-induced vomiting or abusing laxatives, diuretics or enemas. Afterward, they will fall back into a pattern of strictly controlled food intake until they 'lose control' and binge again. I will indicate signs that are specific to any subtype where necessary.

19

Physical Warning Signs

With any illness, mental or physical, there are almost always warning signs that pre-empt a full-blown condition. We ignore warning signs for many reasons, but the main reasons are that we don't know what we are observing, or we are in denial that something is wrong. By recognizing early warning signs that your loved one has anorexia nervosa, you could reduce the impact and minimize the length and brutality of the illness. Don't burden yourself with guilt if you did not recognize warning signs or take action sooner. Anorexia nervosa is a cunning and secretive disease of the mind, and most sufferers go out of their way to be deceptive about their obsession. You can never know for sure what someone else is thinking no matter how close you are to them.

Psychological warning signs include:

- Continued weight loss

- Dizziness and fainting

- Pale skin with sunken eyes

- Feeling cold all the time, even in summer months (poor blood circulation)

- Numbness in the fingers, toes, and face (poor blood circulation)

- Bloating and constipation

- Lethargy

- Irregular sleeping patterns

- Sore muscles

- Recurring muscle cramps

- Chronic headaches

- Recurring infections (compromised immune system)

- Sensitivity and bleeding in the mouth, nose and cracked lips (vitamin deficiency)

- Heart palpitations, chest pains and shortness of breath (anemia)

- The onset of regular bouts of diarrhea or frequent urination (abuse of laxatives or diuretics)

- Swollen jaw from excessive self-induced vomiting (Binge Eating/Purging Subtype)

- Loss or cessation of the menstrual cycle in girls and women

Behavioral and Psychological Warning Signs

There are many behavioral and psychological warning signs as well, but it is unlikely that an anorexic will display all the signs listed. It's more probable that an individual would display a permutation of any of these signs. Remember, anorexics are secretive, so some of the signs could be very subtle, and others may be difficult to identify.

Behavioral warning signs include:

- Changes in eating behavior

- Avoiding (often vehemently) food types that they previously enjoyed

21

- Claiming to have developed food allergies and intolerances

- Counting calories or kilojoules

- Developing ritualistic behaviors around food like eating only foods of one color, insisting on food being placed in certain positions on a plate, eating very slowly, cutting food into very small pieces, refusing to let different foods touch on a plate, etc.

- Displaying extensive knowledge about nutrition, recipes, and food in general

- Preparing elaborate meals for others but refusing to eat any of it

- Eating in private and avoiding shared meals

- Taking up a hobby, or anything similar, that coincides with meal times (a 'valid' excuse to not be present at mealtimes)

- Eliminating certain food types based on nutritional knowledge

- The disappearance of food, evidence of private hoarding of food and of binge eating (Binge Eating/Purging Subtype only)

- Excuses to avoid mealtimes

- Excessive exercising (beyond the norm; exercising when ill, pushing through injury, etc.)

- Becoming anxious if exercise is not possible

- Prioritizing exercising above normal social activities

- Repeated weighing to check body weight

- Constantly speaking about body weight and checking body reflection in a mirror
- Other self-harming behaviors like substance abuse

Psychological warning signs include:

- Becoming anxious, suddenly feeling ill or having to go out around mealtimes
- Rigid thinking around food and weight
- Constantly speaking about being overweight, despite reality being to the contrary
- Denial of hunger, even after going without food for extended periods of time
- Fear of gaining weight
- Regular bouts of depression and anxiety
- Feelings of shame and guilt
- Distorted body image
- Difficulty in concentrating
- Irritability and mood swings
- Low self-esteem
- Dissatisfaction with self
- Social isolation
- Setting unreachable personal goals and constant striving for perfection
- Defensiveness when food, eating, weight or exercise come into the conversation
- In advanced stages, speaking about death

- Contemplating suicide

Physical Complications

The physical complications of anorexia nervosa are far-reaching, and the longer it carries on, the worse they can become. Anorexia nervosa is a life-threatening disease and can be fatal. The physical complications listed below exclude recurrent infections that can take hold and develop into serious medical conditions because of an anorexic's severely compromised immune system.

Physical complications include:

- Anemia
- Vitamin and mineral deficiencies
- Digestive system complications (constipation, diarrhea, hernia, ulcers, etc.)
- Hair loss
- Infertility
- Hormonal and chemical imbalances
- Kidney disease or failure
- Liver disease or failure
- Heart disease or failure
- Swelling of the arms and legs
- Abdominal bloating
- Persistent low blood pressure

• Osteoporosis that leads to bones becoming fragile and fracturing easily

• Development of soft downy hair all over the body, including the face

• Death

All of these complications are treatable and can be healed completely if anorexia nervosa and the resulting conditions are diagnosed in time. Diagnosis depends very much on the anorexic's attitude and whether they are willing to be treated. If an anorexic accepts medical treatment, but secretly continues to limit their food intake the medical treatment will be unsuccessful. Treatment of physiological complications alone is not enough. Medical treatment must be accompanied by psychological treatment as well. If an anorexic is willing to accept medical treatment but declines psychological therapy, relapse is inevitable.

Binge Eating

Binge eating behaviors were first described by American doctor Albert Stunkard in 1959 but were only mentioned in the Diagnostic and Statistical Manual of Mental Disorders (DSM) in 1987 under the criteria of bulimia. Binge eating disorder was separated from bulimia and listed as a different disorder in the DSM-IV published in 1994 within the group of Eating Disorders Not Otherwise Specified. Binge eating disorder was finally categorized as a separate disorder in 2013.

Binge eating disorder is the most common of all eating disorders and is characterized by an ongoing compulsion to eat large volumes of food over a period of around two hours (although that can differ from person to person). Once a binge eater starts eating, they feel overcome by a genuine sense of loss of control and are unable to stop themselves from eating. They are also inclined to eat very fast, often not chewing their food well before swallowing and putting more food in their mouth. Binge eaters will only stop eating when they are uncomfortably full. After a short break, they will eat again even though they are not physically hungry.

Binge eating disorder is accompanied by feelings of anxiety as well as guilt and shame. Feelings of anxiety are often constant, but suffers can feel guilty and ashamed about the amount of food they eat, and the way they eat during binging. They can also feel guilty and ashamed of how they look (overweight or obese) and the fact that their overeating impacts their family. Despite the guilt and shame, they are unable to control their eating. Stress, negative emotions and boredom often trigger binge eating. As the disease progresses, you can see how the emotions of anxiety, as well as guilt and shame, play directly into the initial triggers. Most people with binge eating disorder gradually become more and more antisocial, leading to boredom and loneliness, both of which are triggers for further binge eating, and is characterized by constant episodes of overeating that can happen day or night. The binge eater will eat even if they are not hungry, and make no attempt to get rid of the food through, for example, self-induced vomiting or over-exercise. A sedentary lifestyle more often accompanies binge eating. People with binge eating disorder are usually overweight at best and morbidly obese with poor mobility at worst.

It is very important to note that not all people who are overweight have binge eating disorder.

Also important to note is that not all people with binge eating disorder will eat uncontrollably every day. There are those that do, but others might just binge a few days a week when some internal or external factor triggers the behavior. It is, however, an ongoing pattern of self-destructive behavior.

Each sufferer of binge eating disorder will have their unique reasons for progressing into the disease. There is believed to be a genetic predisposition, and many families have a history of obesity and death related to obesity. In those environments, being overweight is acceptable, and few within the family circle will recognize weight gain as a problem. In fact, many will outright deny constant weight gain as a problem simply because if they do, they will have to address the issues that they choose to avoid.

Mental attitudes towards food and eating can also be passed from parent to child, so if a parent resorts to food for comfort, the child will learn to do the same thing. In many homes, food is also used as a reward, or to distract a child form something. Good grades and other achievements get rewarded with cake, candy or other sweet treats. Likewise, if there is something negative happening, a child can be distracted with a snack. For the most part, this type of reward or distraction is harmless, unless there are pre-existing mental and emotional vulnerabilities that lead to low self-esteem and poor coping skills. In those instances, as the child grows up, it still looks to food for comfort, reward or distraction.

Binge eating disorder is a cunning, secretive mental illness that rapidly brings on physical illness as well. Suffers often go out of their way to hide their eating, and will become very defensive if challenged. If you think your loved one might be suffering from binge eating disorder, confrontation is never a good idea because it will evoke a reactive response of denial and anger. Saying things like "just stop!" or "surely you're not hungry again?" will push the binge eater away and deeper into the secrecy of their disease. Remember, a binge eater is not thinking rationally, and their sense of reality has become warped. If you cannot comprehend, and find anything supportive to say, rather say nothing. Later, if the binge eater goes into treatment, you can speak more openly. While caught up in the dark vortex of eating disorders, all sufferers are lost, emotionally fragile and very vulnerable.

Binge eating disorder occurs across all genders, races, ages, cultures and socioeconomic groups. All sufferers have a distorted sense of reality and an unrealistic mental fixation with food. They also deny the negative physiological symptoms of their obsessive behavior. Their obsession to eat constantly is to the exclusion of any realistic acknowledgment that their actions are causing physical illness. All focus and attention is diverted from physical health and wellbeing and plowed into their obsession with food and eating.

Physical Warning Signs

With any illness, mental or physical, there are almost always warning signs that pre-empt a full-blown condition. We ignore warning signs for many reasons, but the main reasons are that we don't know what we are observing, or we are in denial that something is wrong. By recognizing early warning signs that your loved one has binge eating disorder, you could reduce the impact and minimize the length and brutality of the illness. Don't burden yourself with guilt if you did not recognize warning signs or take action sooner. Binge eating disorder is a cunning and secretive disease of the mind, and most sufferers go out of their way to be deceptive about their obsession. You can never know for sure what someone else is thinking, no matter how close you are to them!

Physiological warning signs include:

• Constant weight gain

• Lethargy

• Irregular sleeping patterns

• Bloating and constipation

• Developing food intolerances

• Nausea and indigestion (from eating too fast)

Behavioral and Psychological Warning Signs

There are many warning behavioral and psychological signs as well, but it is unlikely that a binge eater will display all the signs listed. It's more probable that an

29

individual would display a permutation of any of these signs. Remember, binge eaters are secretive so some of the signs could be very subtle, and others may be difficult to identify.

Behavioral warning signs include:

- Changes in eating behavior
- Overeating to the point of extreme discomfort
- Loss of table manners; gorging on food
- Eating very fast
- Eating large portions of food when not hungry
- Insisting on eating alone
- Eating in secret (hiding binges from family and friends)
- Hoarding food in odd places like a bedroom cupboard for example
- Eating to relieve stress or to calm emotions
- Always claiming to be hungry
- Loss of interest in appearance
- Other self-harming behaviors like substance abuse

Psychological warning signs include:

- Shame and unhappiness about appearance
- Preoccupation food and eating
- Anxiety, shame, guilt and despondency after binging
- Defensiveness to comments about eating, appearance, weight, exercise, etc.

- Depression, anxiety, irritability, and mood swings
- Feeling worthless
- Secretive behavior
- Social isolation
- Defensiveness when food, eating, weight or appearance comes into the conversations
- In advanced stages, speaking about death
- Contemplating suicide

Physical Complications

The physical complications of binge eating disorder are far-reaching, and the longer it carries on, the worse they can become. Binge eating disorder is a life-threatening disease and can be fatal.

- Type 2 Diabetes
- High blood pressure
- High cholesterol
- Stroke
- Kidney disease or failure
- Heart disease or failure
- Gallstones
- Joint and muscle pain
- Osteoarthritis
- Sleep apnoea (interrupted breathing while sleeping)

- Gastrointestinal disease

All of these complications are treatable and healed completely if binge eating disorder and the resulting conditions are diagnosed in time. Diagnosis depends very much on the binge eater's attitude and whether they are willing to be treated. If and binge eater accepts medical treatment, but secretly continues to binge on food, the medical treatment will be unsuccessful. Treatment of physiological complications alone is not enough. Medical treatment must be accompanied by psychological treatment as well. If a binge eater is willing to accept medical treatment but declines psychological therapy, relapse is inevitable.

Bulimia Nervosa

In previous centuries Bulimia nervosa was recognized, but it was thought to be a physical disease due to some medical condition. In the early 1900's French psychologist and psychotherapist, Pierre Marie Felix Janet published a paper that began discussing symptoms of bulimia nervosa, but little was known of the condition. In 1979 English psychiatrist Gerald Francis Morris Russell published a paper describing cases and treatments for bulimia nervosa. He distinguished bulimia nervosa from anorexia nervosa in a subsequent paper and published further studies in 2004 that led to bulimia being recognized as a separate disorder.

Recurrent bouts of binge eating characterize bulimia nervosa followed immediately afterward by attempts to rid the body (purging) of what has been eaten by self-induced vomiting, or abusing laxatives, diuretics or enemas. Bulimics also place excessive emphasis on body shape or weight. Self-esteem and self-worth are defined by the way they look.

Binge eating can be defined as an ongoing compulsion to eat large volumes of food over a period of around two hours, and once a binge starts bulimics are overcome by a genuine sense of loss of control and are unable to stop themselves from eating.

A bulimia nervosa sufferer can become caught up in an uncontrollable cycle of binge eating and purging to rid the body of what has been eaten. This is a very dangerous and life-threatening cycle that can lead to physical illness and death. Unfortunately, these behaviors become out of control and compulsive over time and lead to obsessions with food, eating, weight loss, and body image.

All bulimia nervosa sufferers have a distorted self-image. They have a mental fixation with their body that does not correlate realistically with the facts. They also deny the negative physiological symptoms of their obsessive behavior. Their obsession with controlling weight loss is to the exclusion of any realistic acknowledgment that their actions are causing physical illness. All focus and attention is diverted from physical health and wellbeing and plowed into their obsession with losing and keeping weight off.

Not all bulimia nervosa sufferers have dramatic weight loss. Some maintain a normal weight, others might be slightly underweight, and some appear slightly overweight. That, combined with the cunning and secretive nature of bulimia nervosa and the fact that sufferers will go to extreme lengths to hide their condition, can lead to the problem going unnoticed for a long time.

Triggers of bulimia nervosa are similar to those of anorexia nervosa, and each sufferer will have their unique reasons for progressing into the disease. There is believed to be a genetic predisposition, and environmental and social factors can weigh in strongly as well. As with anorexia nervosa, it can be triggered by dieting and exercise to meet society's norms, but for dieting and weight loss to become a destructive obsession, there has to be a pre-existing mental and emotional vulnerability that leads to low self-esteem. Some sufferers fall into a binge/purge obsession to feel in control of their body weight. This is mostly because there are areas of their life that they believe they cannot control. Having control over their body weight, no matter how distorted their impressions, gives them a sense of power over a life that is dominated by powerlessness (genuine or perceived). Many triggers are subtle and difficult to expose and understand, but all will center around anxiety, low self-esteem, and poor coping skills.

If you suspect that your loved one suffers from bulimia nervosa, don't challenge them; not even lovingly. Saying things like "why do you do that? It's awful!" or "what's wrong with you?" will push the bulimic away and deeper into the secrecy of their disease. Remember, a bulimic is not thinking rationally, and their sense of reality has become warped. If you cannot comprehend and find anything supportive to say, rather say nothing. Later, if the bulimic goes into treatment, you can speak more openly. While caught up in the dark vortex of eating disorders, all sufferers are lost, emotionally fragile and very vulnerable.

Physical Warning Signs

With any illness, mental or physical, there are almost always warning signs that pre-empt a full-blown condition. We ignore warning signs for many reasons, but the main reasons are that we don't know what we are observing, or we are in denial that something is wrong. By recognizing early warning signs that your loved one has bulimia nervosa, you could reduce the impact and minimize the length and brutality of the illness. Don't burden yourself with guilt if you did not recognize warning signs or take action sooner. Bulimia nervosa is a cunning and secretive disease of the mind, and most sufferers go out of their way to be deceptive about their obsession. You can never know for sure what someone else is thinking no matter how close you are to them.

Physiological warning signs include:

- Ongoing fluctuation in weight
- Dizziness and fainting
- Bloating and constipation
- Lethargy
- Irregular sleeping patterns
- Sore muscles
- Recurring muscle cramps (dehydration)

- Chronic headaches (dehydration)

- Recurring infections (compromised immune system)

- Sensitivity and bleeding in the mouth, nose and cracked lips (vitamin deficiency)

- Swollen jaw from excessive self-induced vomiting (irritation caused by stomach acid)

- Recurring throat infections

- Callouses on knuckles (damage by teeth during bouts of self-induced vomiting)

- Tooth erosion and bad breath (stomach acid erodes tooth enamel)

- Heart palpitations, chest pains and shortness of breath (anemia)

- The onset of regular bouts of diarrhea or frequent urination (abuse of laxatives or diuretics)

- Loss or cessation of the menstrual cycle in girls and women

Behavioral and Psychological Warning Signs

There are many behavioral and psychological warning signs as well, but it is unlikely that a bulimic will display all the signs listed. It's more probable that an individual would display a permutation of any of these signs. Remember, bulimics are secretive, so some of the signs could be very subtle, and others may be difficult to identify.

Behavioral warning signs include:

• Changes in eating behavior

• Eating in secret (hiding binges from family and friends)

• Avoiding eating with other people

• Disappearance of food, evidence of private hoarding of food and binge eating

• Secretive or erratic behavior around food

• Constant dieting (counting calories/kilojoules, avoiding fats or carbohydrates, etc.)

• Using appetite suppressants, laxatives, diuretics or enemas to lose weight, and justifying their value

• Excessive exercising (beyond the norm; exercising when ill, pushing through injury, etc.)

• Becoming anxious if exercise is not possible

• Prioritizing exercising above normal social activities

• Repeated weighing to check body weight

• Constantly speaking about body weight and checking body reflection in a mirror

• Frequent trips to the toilet or bathroom during or just after meals (evidence of purging or laxative use)

• Other self-harming behaviors like substance abuse

Psychological warning signs include:

• Rigid thinking around food and weight

- Constantly speaking about being overweight, despite reality being to the contrary
- Fear of gaining weight
- Obsession with food, and a need to control food
- Regular bouts of depression and anxiety
- Difficulty in concentrating
- Distorted body image
- Irritability and mood swings
- Low self-esteem
- Feelings of shame and guilt
- Dissatisfaction with self
- Social isolation
- Setting unreachable personal goals and constant striving for perfection
- Defensiveness when food, eating, weight or exercise comes into the conversation
- In advanced stages, speaking about death
- Contemplating suicide

Physical Complications

The physical complications of bulimia nervosa are far-reaching, and the longer it carries on, the worse they can become. Bulimia nervosa is a life-threatening disease and can be fatal.

- Indigestion, heartburn and gastric reflux

- Chronic throat inflammation and infections

- Inflammation and potential rupture of the esophagus caused by persistent vomiting

- Stomach and intestinal ulcers

- Chronic complications of the gastrointestinal system due to laxative abuse

- Irregular heartbeat that can lead to heart disease

- Osteoporosis that leads to bones becoming fragile and fracturing easily

- Infertility

All of these complications are treatable and can be healed completely if bulimia nervosa and the resulting conditions are diagnosed in time. Diagnosis depends very much on the bulimic's attitude and whether they are willing to be treated. If a bulimic accepts medical treatment, but secretly continues to limit their food intake the medical treatment will be unsuccessful. Treatment of physiological complications alone is not enough. Medical treatment must be accompanied by psychological treatment as well. If an anorexic is willing to accept medical treatment but declines psychological therapy, relapse is inevitable.

Other Specified Feeding or Eating Disorder

Other Specified Feeding or Eating Disorder (OSFED), or Eating Disorder Not Otherwise Specified (EDNOS) encompasses recognized eating disorders that display many of the symptoms of Anorexia Nervosa, Bulimia Nervosa, and Binge Eating Disorder, but do not meet the full criteria of symptoms of any specific eating disorder for a complete diagnosis.

Being diagnosed with OSFED does not mean that the person does not have a very serious and potentially fatal mental illness that has led to serious physiological complications. OSFED criteria for who is susceptible, and it affects people just as the three recognized eating disorders do. Causes and triggers are as diverse as for recognized eating disorders.

The warning signs of OSFED will be found among the warning signs o the three recognized eating disorders in a variety of combinations and permutations. OSFED can also fluctuate to extremes between the recognized disorders. These warning signs will point to a person with an extremely disturbing attitude towards food and eating, and a distorted body image.

Being aware of the warning signs of the three recognized eating disorders will help you to establish if your loved one has OSFED. It is accepted that if someone repeatedly displays any of a combination of the physiological, behavioral and psychological warning signs of any of the recognized eating disorders for three months or more, they have a problem that must be addressed with professional help. Because of the medical complications that accompany all eating disorders, professional help should be received sooner rather than later.

Unfortunately, that is not always possible because of the cunning and secretive nature of all eating disorders. Again, don't try to confront your loved one if your suspect OSFED. Approaching the subject must be handled with sensitivity because if your suspicions are right, you will be met with vehement denial. Remember, anyone with an eating disorder is not thinking rationally and their sense of reality has become warped. While caught up in the dark vortex of eating disorders, all sufferers are lost, emotionally fragile and very vulnerable. You don't want to push your loved one away.

Can Eating Disorders be Prevented?

There are preventative factors that can potentially reduce the likelihood of someone developing an eating disorder, but there is no scientific proof that eating disorders can are preventable. Possible preventative factors have been divided into three groups: individual, family and socio-cultural.

Preventative factors are listed as:

Individual preventative skills:

- High self-esteem
- Positive body image
- Strong sense of emotional wellbeing
- Does well at school/tertiary education
- Independent and assertive
- Good social skills
- Able to perform multiple social roles
- Solid problem-solving skills
- Solid coping skills

Family preventative skills:

• Belonging to a family that does not place emphasis on physical appearance

• Belonging to a family that does not level internal or external criticism

• Eating regular family meals together

Socio-cultural preventative skills:

• Belonging to a culture other than Western culture; other cultures are more accepting of physical appearance and place more emphasis on inner qualities

• Involvement in an industry that places little emphasis on physical appearance; laid back working environment and culture where skill is valued above appearance

• Peer and social support structures and relationships that place little emphasis on physical appearance

None of these points is guaranteed to prevent an eating disorder developing, and there is little scientific or psychological proof to support these points.

Chapter 2

Confronting Eating Disorders

If you suspect your loved one has an eating order, you could be right. If you are right, then your loved one needs professional help as soon as possible. It all seems quite clear, and you should be able to resolve the issue very easily – but not will obsessive behaviors triggered by mental illness.

If you are right, you must know upfront that you have no control over the situation, even if your loved one is a minor. You definitely can influence the person positively, but you have no control over them or their eating disorder. Likewise, you can influence the person negatively and drive them deeper into mental illness by trying to impose your will. Accepting this puts you in a very good position mentally and emotionally.

Some people refuse to accept that eating disorders are not a lifestyle choice and that the sufferer is just difficult. Many people see eating disorders as an attempt to get attention. None of this is true of course, but if you have a close family member who holds these or similar views, it is very important that you encourage them to distance themselves from the sufferer while you are trying to encourage openness about the problem. Eating disorders are not easy to understand let alone accept. That does not mean that anyone has to move out or that there need be any negative feelings, it just means that there must be mutual respect. An agreement to steer clear of your attempts to engage with the sufferer about the reality of their condition.

This is particularly important if the sufferer is a minor. A minor depends on your home for survival, and it's unlikely that they can easily go and live somewhere else. You must not allow the minor to become alienated in their own home; that could be disastrous! It is very easy for a negative group mentality to revolve around something that people don't understand. So a parent, grandparent or important family member that refuses to acknowledge an eating disorder as a problem can negatively influence other family members and siblings. It can make the sufferer feel rejected and ostracised by their family. Feelings like this cut very deep, and leave deep psychological scars that can negatively affect the person's ability to trust and have healthy relationships throughout their life.

All eating disorders have at their core anxiety, poor coping skills, and low self-esteem. If confronted with aggression, ridicule or disdain the sufferer will withdraw into their problem and shy away from any attempts by anyone to reach out to them. The negative emotions that come from aggression, ridicule or disdain could also drive the sufferer to other self-destructive behaviors like substance abuse in an attempt to cope.

Approaching the Problem

Choosing the right time to address your concerns is vital if you are going to make any headway. Mealtime is the worst time to address an eating disorder because the person is already going to be anxious. Also choosing to broach the subject in front of other people can make the sufferer feel vulnerable and as if people are ganging up on them. If you another loved one want to broach the subject together, make sure that you are all prepared and that you make it clear from the start that you are all concerned, and that you are not ganging up.

If there have been recent confrontations and arguments, give it a day or two before you try to discuss the problem. Wait for hurt emotions to calm down and be restored because you would just be wasting your time if you don't. You don't want the discussion to degenerate into a back and forth blame game, with tears and anger. When you are mentally and emotionally prepared, choose a time when there will be no distractions, and you can speak in private. You have to be the stronger and more mature person in the discussion, so you have to draw on all your patience, love and wisdom to steer the conversation productively.

Do:

- Explain that you love the person and that is why you are concerned

- Refer to specific behaviors without condemnation

- Explain why these behaviors concern you

- Tell them of the health complications with compassion

- Tell the person that you don't want them to suffer, and you don't want them to die

- Keep the conversation flowing from both sides, and listen to the responses

- Tell the person that you don't understand if that is the case, but reassure them that you want to help them

- Open sentences with "I" as in "I love you and want to help you" rather than "you" as in "you are harming yourself, and that worries me". "You" carries an accusing tone.

- Avoid speaking about food; focus on the person and their feelings

- Encourage them to open up to you and tell you how they feel

- Accept what they say and don't deny their words, for example, if they say "I feel unloved" don't retort with "that's ridiculous! You know we all love you". Instead, try something like "I didn't know that. Why do you feel unloved?"

- Listen to how they feel and avoid telling them how you feel.

• Offer solutions, and if the conversation is going well, raise seeking professional help together

Don't:

• Come in guns blazing

• Threaten or set ultimatums

• Speak over them to get your point across

• Lecture and tell the person how they feel

• Manipulate by trying to elicit guilt: "what about the family?" or "I have tried so hard."

• Turn the situation around: "what have we done that you are like this?"

• Comment on their appearance: "you used to be so beautiful/handsome."

• Shame: "aren't you ashamed of how much you eat/ how thin you are/ what you look like"

• Accuse: "you are harming yourself/you will end up killing yourself."

• Belittle: "can't you control yourself?" or "just stop this foolishness."

You cannot expect to have one conversation, and everything will come right. That is unrealistic, and you will end up feeling disappointed. Rather view the first conversation as one of many to come before your loved one admits and surrenders to their problem. If the first conversation went well, keep working on building trust, but don't try to discuss the problem again for a few days.

If your loved one raises the problem, however, be willing to discuss it. See it as a type of grooming process.

Coping with Denial and Anger

Despite your best attempts, there is a very good possibility that your attempts to approach the problem will be met with denial and anger. If this happens, you will have to do your level best to keep calm and allow your loved one to speak their mind. If you can keep calm, it could be quite helpful to listen to what they say. They could disclose issues of how they feel that you were previously unaware of.

Whatever you do, don't allow the situation to spiral out of control. You don't have to get your point across. Rather walk away and resolve to try again on another day.

Do:

- Keep calm

- Reassure: "I understand that you are angry/upset."

- Reaffirm your motivation: "I want to help you" or "I want to understand."

- Comfort: "I know you are afraid."

- Listen carefully to what is being said without countering anything

- Leave the conversation if emotions are becoming too heated

- Say something like "let's discuss this another time" before you leave

48

Don't

- Get angry and retaliate to comments
- Threaten and condemn
- Shout the person down
- Accuse

Denial is a very strong emotion. Anger fuels denial and anger in this situation is fuelled by guilt. None of these has anything to do with you. It is your loved one's own inner turmoil that is being driven by a problem that they have no control over. It is vital that you understand that so that you can successfully disengage your ego and emotions from the situation. It is not about you, although it might be directed at you. This is where your courage and maturity must step to the fore.

Denial and the resulting anger is in no way a sign of giving up hope. It is a clear sign that your loved one feels overwhelmed by their situation and does not believe that they have the skills to cope with the enormity of what stands before them. Their anxiety is an indication that they feel that what you are asking of them is greater than what they can offer in return.

Ignorance can also elicit denial and guilt. Your loved one knows what is happening in their life, they believe that they cannot cope with the situation and they probably fear the consequences. But they can see no way out. This is particularly true if their disease has advanced and there are physiological complications at play. We all fear death! Knowing that you can die because of your behavior and actions is scary. Believing that your self-destructive

49

behavior and actions are inescapable can be terrifying. Many people with eating disorders resign themselves to death while caught up in the grip of mental illness. They just cannot see a way out.

Working your way through your loved one's anger and denial will take time, patience, wisdom and courage but both of you can get through the void if you persist. It is very important that you take good care of yourself at a time like this. You cannot pour from an empty cup! Make sure that you get enough rest and that you eat well. Also, it is a good idea to join a support group or find a therapist yourself so that you can express your feelings and be heard.

Are you an Enabler?

Enablers are more prevalent around people with bulimia nervosa and binge eating disorder than around people with anorexia nervosa, however, anorexia nervosa is not immune. A person with an eating disorder finds an enabler in someone who supports and encourages their self-destructive behavior. The enabler believes that they are protecting the person from the consequences of their lifestyle, but in fact, their actions allow the person with the eating disorder to sink deeper into their problem. The enabler believes that they do what they are doing out of love, but their love becomes their own, and their loved one's downfall. Enablers learn to accept the unacceptable and blur the boundaries between right and wrong. They will lie together with their loved one, denying self-destructive behavior patterns. It is common in treatment that an enabler will deny truths that can prove that the person with an eating disorder is not keeping to an eating plan. Some enablers will go as far as to sneak food to people with bulimia nervosa or binge eating disorder while they are being treated in a hospital or a rehabilitation center.

The person with an eating disorder learns to rely on the enabler, often believing that they are entitled to the enabler's support and protection. The enabler becomes completely caught up in their loved one's lifestyle, often putting their own needs, health and welfare at risk to support and protect their loved one. It is not uncommon for an enabler to give up work to take care of someone who has binge eating disorder. In these cases the enabler accepts full responsibility for their loved one's care, being on call twenty-four hours a day to prepare food, buy food, bathe and clean up after their loved one. In some cases, the enabler is a child, which means that the child grows up with a warped sense of reality, and their future prospects are stymied from an early age.

Are you an enabler?

Do you:

• Regularly give a bulimic or binge eater money or buy food for them?

• Do you prepare food for a binge eater while they are binging?

• Do you prepare or buy food for a binge eater even after you have been told not to by a medical practitioner?

51

- Do you choose to look the other way rather than confront the fact that your loved one's self-destructive behavior is killing them?

- Do you explain away an anorexic or bulimic's weight problems or health issues?

- Do you lie for your loved one if people question their behavior (binge eating, purging, etc.)?

- Do you accept the unacceptable regarding your loved one's behavior?

- Do you trivialize serious issues and sweep matters under the carpet?

An enabler needs professional help and support. If you think that you are an enabler, you must get professional counseling to separate you from your loved ones eating disorder. By protecting your loved one from the consequences of their self-destructive lifestyle you are not helping them, and it is highly unlikely that they will ever confront their problem.

Many enablers have some level of psychological problems themselves. It could stem from many past issues in their life ranging from fear, or a dysfunctional childhood that left them without proper coping skills, to having had a parent who enabled a spouse or child. Sometimes it is best that a person with an eating disorder and the enabler be separated from each other for a while for both of their sake. This separation will allow both to deal with issues like guilt and detachment issues.

The enabler must also learn to put their own needs, health, and welfare first. They must rebuild their self-confidence, self-esteem and learn to enjoy life again. Under professional guidance, the enabler will be educated on the causes of eating disorders, the behavior of sufferers and the Three C's that anyone close to a sufferer of eating disorders must understand: you did not Cause it; you cannot Cure it; you cannot control it!

Are you Co-Dependent?

What sets co-dependency apart from enabling? Co-dependency can be defined as having an excessive emotional or psychological reliance on a partner, typically one with an illness or addiction who requires support. Co-dependency includes obsessive, compulsive behavior patterns and actions, and the cause of this is also rooted in deep-set psychological problems.

A co-dependent on the surface wants to save the suffering, but beneath the surface, there are many and wide-ranging issues that spurn them on to keep the situation as it is, like insecurity, control, power, and even ego. As with many psychological issues, the co-dependent may be unaware of the subconscious issues that plague them.

To briefly touch on the four underlying psychological issues mentioned:

Insecurity in a relationship leads to a need to be sure that your partner or child will never leave. In partner relationships, this could be triggered by past experiences and fear of abandonment. An insecure co-dependent may be subjected to severe abuse by their loved one, but they will continue to support them, 'love' them and try to cure them because they believe that they cannot live without the person. In parent/child relationships the parent may fear not having anyone to look after and nurture anymore; the fear of the 'empty nest syndrome'. Where children are caught up taking care of a parent with an eating disorder, the situation usually evolves, with mostly one child getting caught up in their parent's self-destructive lifestyle. The child becomes the caregiver and because they know nothing else, they become fearful of the thought that their parent could die and leave them behind. These children resist change out of fear and insecurity. They mostly know no other way of life.

As a result of the underlying fear, control comes into play and ties in with insecurity in any relationship." You cannot leave me if I am in control of you!" Power also plays a role in co-dependent relationships, and the power usually rests with the one who has money. A child who lives with a parent and has no income of their own is in their parent's control because the parent provides a safe home, and has the power to give or withhold money. A person who is suffering from an eating disorder, and does not work but earns a state grant has power over a co-dependent child, parent or partner that does not earn their own income. Without the sufferer to co-dependent has no home or means to live.

These are only some of the psychological issues that lie behind co-dependency, and the examples given are mere guidelines of what could be driving the co-dependent. Codependents are behavioral addicts, ranging from desperate to very dangerous. All co-dependents need professional help, but few will ever seek it because their problem is a behavioral dependence and they are unable to identify with that concept.

Chapter 3

What if your Loved One is a Minor

Peer pressure plays a major role in a minor's self-esteem. Being accepted by peers is very important, and Smartphones and social media have accentuated the need to be seen and accepted. Social media groups and selfies are the norm, and 'likes' are a vital social pillar to an immature mind. Another obvious negative influence on self-esteem is where children come from dysfunctional homes and are witness to, or subjected to abuse and criticism on a regular basis.

Changes in a minor's eating behavior will be quite obvious if you are an attentive parent who shares mealtimes with your family. If you don't or are unable to share mealtimes with your family the changes might not immediately be obvious. All eating disorders are by nature a secretive and cunning disease, and a minor could easily evade attention. This is very important to remember because you have to trust people who are close to you to have healthy relationships. If you do not identify changes in eating behavior before the disease has progressed, you must not feel guilty. There is no wrong in trusting someone and believing their excuses.

The most important thing is that once you realize that your child has an eating disorder, you must not react with shock, horror, and blame. Also, don't become defensive. Having a child with an eating disorder is not a reflection of you, your parenting skills or the family dynamics so don't react as if it is. Rather choose to respond by learning as much as you can about eating disorders as soon as possible. Find a support group and speak to a therapist. Research and read as much as you can on the subject. This will allow you to go through the long road of recovery with support and understanding.

Educate your partner, other children, and family members. Explain eating disorders to them and encourage them to support you and your child. If any family member is averse to the problem, particularly seeing as it is a mental illness, ask them to not aggravate the situation and the step back from the sufferer until you have made progress.

When you approach the problem with your child, use the same guidelines as in the earlier subchapter: "Approaching the Problem'. Remember that you are the adult and you don't have a mental illness. Patience and maturity are vital if you want to make progress. You must expect tears and tantrums at first when you are trying to get your child to acknowledge that they have an eating disorder. Also, bear in mind that your child might not understand what an eating disorder is. No one goes into anything with the intention of having an eating disorder; a mental illness! There is no glory in that, only shame and fear. Remember, being accepted in very important to minors so admitting to a disease of the mind, which broader society finds unacceptable and many reject outright, is not an easy ask for anyone let alone a minor.

If you come to a point where you can discuss the problem calmly with your child, the first thing you must do is promise your support, and the second thing is that you will keep it private. Many people and minors, in particular, are willing to go into therapy and seek medical help if they have the support of someone who loves them and they know that it will be kept away from other people. Getting a minor into treatment is vital because their bodies are still developing and eating disorders can wreak havoc that could lead to permanent, and chronic health issues like kidney failure or infertility, but it must be done by winning trust and through gentle persuasion. That is why it is always beneficial to get the support of the whole family, but where that is not possible the love and support of just one other person are good enough to begin the journey of recovery.

At no point must you assume the role of the demanding parent who lays down the law and gets your child into a rehabilitation center or outpatient treatment under force. You can do it! You have the right as a parent to force your child into professional care, but the damage done will be massive. You will lose your child's trust, and even if they do recover, they could hold your actions against you for years. You want your child to trust you and agree to seek professional help. If they buy into recovery right from the start, successful recovery is more likely.

Parents can Play a Role in Influencing their Child's Choices

The prime role of parenting would be to raise your child to have a positive self-image, realistic view of life and trust you enough to be able to discuss challenging or embarrassing subjects with you. This comes from openly showing love, spending quality time with your child, not speaking at them - but with them, listening to their opinions, asking them how their day went and how they feel, allowing them to make choices and guiding them if their choice is not the best, laughing with your child and always staying interested and in-touch with your child.

This sounds like straightforward parenting, but in the real world of financial pressures, work stresses, marriage problems, divorce and the myriad of daily challenges parents face it is very easy to begin living past your child. Without realizing, your child could begin to feel lonely and isolated.

A child raised in a trusting and loving environment is more likely to build a positive self-image and solid coping skills. Adolescence, in particular, is a time when a child who feels vulnerable, ignored or inadequate can very easily develop anxiety disorders. If you are living past your child, you may not notice the early warning signs and will, therefore, have little chance of excerpting any influence over your child later on.

The evolution from child to adult that we all experience in adolescence is a time of great chemical and hormonal changes in our physiology, and confusion and insecurity as we navigate mental changes. A child in a loving and supportive family environment can cope with these changes because they know that they have the necessary emotional support.

The only skill that we are all born with is an innate survival skill. All other skills have to be taught or learned from the people and the environment surrounding us throughout our development. One of the major factors contributing to a partiality to anxiety-based mental illness that is not genetically predisposed is poor coping skills. Even if a person has a susceptibility to obsessive behaviors, but is raised in a loving, supportive environment that equips them with solid coping skills, they may never develop an anxiety-based mental illness

If you as a parent display poor coping skills that is what you will teach your child! Poor coping skills will exacerbate stress and anxiety, and the inclination to 'medicate' long-term stress through unhealthy compulsive behavioral patterns has been proven time and again in countless studies conducted worldwide.

Think of a bird being kept in a small cage or on its own without attention. Feather plucking becomes a common behavior pattern. A dog kept on its own without any attention will display unhealthy behavioral patterns like ceaseless barking or falling into depression. The same applies to any animals, birds or reptiles that are, for example, kept in overcrowded conditions; fighting to the death and even cannibalism becomes the norm. All of these behavior patterns are alien to the species when they live in their natural environment or are kept as pets that have adequate space and companionship.

Humans are no different! When there is too much stress and anxiety something has to give, and we begin finding coping mechanisms. These are often substance unhealthy and compulsive behavior patterns.

Apart from good parenting and loving attachments to your child, get into the habit of:

•   Showing daily interest in your child's activities and sharing your day with your child

•   Be open to discussing drug and alcohol abuse, sexual issues, etc. with your child; TV programs watched together can often be an initiator (especially true crime programs)

•   Tell your child that you love them and encourage them to reciprocate; make hugs a standard

•   Share your life with your child by:

o   Sharing your childhood and adolescent years

o   Admit that you made mistakes and struggled with some issues

o   Tell them what you learned from your mistakes and how you resolved issues

o   Discuss your hopes and future ambitions

•   Share family problems with your child, don't hide them by:

o	Admitting to indiscretions in the extended family if there are (like the uncle in jail)

o	Explaining that we are not responsible for what happens to other family members

o	Avoiding the 'family secret' syndrome that leads to hidden shame

o	Openly discussing the circumstances if you are separated from your child's father/mother, explaining the reasons without anger or bitterness

o	Not running your previous partner down; your relationship with them is not comparable with the relationship your child may have with them

o	Reassuring your child that the separation was in no way their fault

o	Allowing your child to ask questions and answer them honestly

o	Speaking about death, the of a loved one; many people think it caring to shield a child from the reality of death - it's not, it just leaves the child confused

•	Allow your child to share their life with you by:

o	Encouraging open discussion

o	Not overreacting if something they say sounds dicey

o	Listening to understand and then discuss the issue

o	Not arguing and try to persuade; rather explain and make yourself clear

o	Looking to understand your child's feelings and emotions

o   Acknowledging that they have been heard and give reassurance

•   Appreciate your child and encourage (not demand) reciprocal appreciation by:

o   Acknowledging positive changes and behavior

o   Guiding your child if they stray or don't understand; be firm, but not harsh

o   Saying thank-you and showing appreciation for jobs well done and acts of care or kindness

o   Not taking anything for granted

o   Praising your child for doing things that deserve praise

•   Discuss the world around you and identify life values together by:

o   Identifying your family values

o   Asking your child what they view as good and bad values

o   Discussing the impact of good and bad values on individuals, family, and society

•   Your actions show that you care; lead by example by:

o   Setting limits and keeping to your limits

o   Avoiding a 'do as I say and not as I do' mentality; it will be likely met with revolt

o   Being consistent with your values, limits, standards and giving love and praise

- Teach your child mutual respect by:

o   Not blaming and shaming them (in private or in front of others)

o   Not comparing your child negatively to other people; we are all individuals

o   Listening to their side and then calmly giving your side; encourage resolution

o   Not prying or setting your child up; this is disrespectful and breaks trust

o   Teaching your child self-reliance and independence; give them rope with boundaries

o   Making your child accept responsibility for their actions or inactions

o   Explaining the consequences of not taking responsibility and letting your child experience the consequences in a firm but supportive way

Encourage a healthy lifestyle, not only for your child but yourself and the rest of the family. Participate in joint activities like outdoor sports, hobbies like art or music, welcome your child's suggestions and make these activities a regular part of your weekly routines.

Of course, despite all your efforts your child can still hide stress and anxiety and develop unhealthy compulsive behavioral patterns like an eating disorder. There is one definite fact though if your child develops an eating disorder, sufferers who go into recovery and come from loving and supportive families stand a higher chance of long-term recovery than those who do not come from a stable and supportive family background.

Chapter 4

After the Diagnosis

Once your loved one has been diagnosed with an eating disorder, it is important that you prepare yourself for what lies ahead by doing as much research as you can. You can also join online support groups, and if there is a face to face support group in your area, join them as well. Support groups are a wonderful source of comfort and information. Many people in the group will have experienced what you are going through, and they can offer invaluable guidance and insight.

When your loved one is first diagnosed with an eating disorder, expect yourself to feel a broad range of emotions ranging from shock, confusion, denial, anger, and guilt. Accept your feelings; they are normal. Once reality sinks in, and you think more clearly you can start taking positive action.

Expect to feel:

• Very distressed about the situation, your loved one's wellbeing and the wellbeing of the whole family.

• Confused about what you can do, or how you can help

• Fear that your loved one can die, and also fear about physiological damage already done

• A loss of interest in daily life and things that you used to enjoy

• Fear about meal times and food in general

• Anxious about how you will handle treatment and the future

• Disappointed in yourself and your loved one

• Frustrated because you don't know how to change the circumstances

• Hopeless that things will ever come right

Understanding Eating Disorders

Research into eating disorders is in its infancy, and there is not very much proven research available. What is clear is that eating disorders are a set of very complicated and complex conditions that together contribute to the development of the condition.

Eating disorders can develop at any age and are not selective. Some studies have indicated teenage girls to be most susceptible to developing anorexia nervosa and bulimia nervosa, and different studies attribute susceptibility of the same two conditions to women over thirty, so a lot of research must still be done. There are however certain external presiding factors that professionals believe can predict the potential for someone to develop an eating disorder.

It is not an exact science, but if you study the contributing factors, it becomes obvious that eating disorders are complicated and dangerous. With so many contributing factors and facets to the disease, treatment understandably has to be ongoing and in-depth to firstly uncover the underlying causes, and then address them sufficiently to bring about rehabilitation.

It is also a fact that eating disorders run in families, but science has yet to prove if it is nature or nurture that has eating disorders run from one generation to another.

Whatever the underlying causes and triggers, eating disorders are not a whim of vanity. They are a very serious mental illness that causes physiological complications that can lead to death. When in the throes of their mental illness, someone suffering from an eating disorder has no control over their condition; they are powerless over their psychology and biology. That is why professional intervention is essential. Eating disorders often also develop along with other conditions like depression, anxiety disorders and substance abuse that makes recovery even more of an uphill battle.

Contributing Factors

Contributing factors or risk factors are external situations that are present before the onset of an eating disorder and can potentially predict that a person might be vulnerable to developing an eating disorder. Any factor can be present for a period of time in a person's life or be an ongoing presence. The factors have been combined and not isolated to any specific eating disorder because very few studies have been conducted, and nothing is as yet proven, but rather only indicated as a potential factor.

Contributing factors include:

- Low self-esteem
- Poor coping skills
- Anxiety
- Feeling inadequate
- Separation from parents for an extended period
- Eating alone
- Social pressure around being thin/muscular
- Idealizing the 'perfect body.'
- Internalising being thin as being best
- Being overweight as a child
- Social norms that judge on appearance and place little value on inner qualities
- Social norms that criticize and prejudice weight, appearance, race, etc.

- Being surrounded by a negative attitude towards food
- Being surrounded by negative comments about eating
- Childhood conflicts around mealtimes (a child who refuses to eat and it causes stress)
- Eating very little during childhood and puberty
- Fussy and selective eating in childhood
- Perfectionism and a strong desire to achieve
- Constant dieting (adopting dieting as a way of life)
- Regular fasting and skipping meals
- Depression in childhood or adolescence
- Loneliness at any age
- History of being teased excessively or bullied
- Difficulty expressing emotions or feelings
- History of physical, emotional or sexual abuse

Research is currently being conducted into the genetic predisposition to eating disorders around an imbalance in chemicals in the brain that controls hunger, appetite, and digestion. In some people with eating disorders, these chemicals have been found to be unbalanced, but research has not yet proven a direct connection with developing eating disorders. Eating disorders also tend to run in families, but as yet no other genetic or chemical factor has been isolated.

Other factors are being researched to confirm that they have a link to developing eating disorders. These include:

- Premature birth

- A low birth weight

- Multiple births (one of)

- A complicated or difficult birth

- Cephalohematoma: a traumatic hematoma that occurs underneath the skin in the dense layer of vascular tissue over an infant's skull bone. It does not pose any risk to brain cells but causes pooling of blood. It can be caused by:

o   Forceps being used during birthing

o   First pregnancy

o   Difficult a prolonged labor

o   Infant's head being bigger than the mother's pelvic area

If you suspect that your loved one has an eating disorder and you recognize any combination of factors mentioned above as playing a role in your loved one's life, your fears could be founded. If your loved one has been diagnosed with an eating disorder and you recognize any combination of the factors mentioned above as playing a role in your loved one's life, it will help you gain a deeper understanding of the situation.

Coping with the Diagnosis

If you love someone who has an eating disorder, know upfront that you are in for a long haul; there are no shortcuts!

But coping with reality depends on how difficult you want to make it for yourself. You have to accept that it is your loved one's problem and not yours, even if they are a minor. As blunt as that sounds, it's a fact. If you want your loved one to recover, but they don't want to recover you are powerless over the situation.

Having a loved one who has an eating disorder is going to cause you a lot of emotional pain, and most probably over a long period. It is very important that you face your emotional pain head-on and deal with it. The fact is, the outcome of setbacks we experience in life depends on how we react to them rather than on what happened. Walkthrough your emotional pain. Process what has happened, understand how or why it happened, and then accept what has happened and move on.

Yes, you might fall apart for a while. Your life might be turned upside-down for a while. You will cry. You will feel depressed. You will feel guilty. You will blame yourself. You will feel as if the emotional pain is endless. But the greatest cause of ongoing emotional pain is resistance to what happened. By resisting the diagnosis, you will deny yourself acceptance. Without acceptance, you will not be able to make progress.

Remember, in life, nothing is promised, and nothing is guaranteed. We attach expectations to how we think our life should be, and then we believe in these expectations.

We will our lives in our direction, and we want to control. When life does not go along with our expectations, we feel hurt and angry. The greater the gap between your expectations and reality, the greater your stress and emotional pain will be. No parent, child or partner expects their loved one to be diagnosed with an eating disorder, and neither did you. Walking through emotional pain to ultimately understand and accept closes the gap between expectation and reality. You will realize that the eating disorder is not, and never was in your control. As you realize this, you will free yourself from the emotions of guilt, anger, and fear and you will be able to focus on the reality of the situation.

There are two realities to loving someone with an eating disorder, and you will have to cope with one, or even both at different stages in the process. The first would be having your suspicions confirmed, and your loved one agrees to professional treatment. Or, having your suspicions confirmed, and your loved one stays in denial and refuses treatments. Most people who are in denial will insist that they can heal themselves after they have been diagnosed. So the person does not deny that they have an eating disorder, but they deny that they need professional medical or psychological help.

Both of these situations are extremely challenging, exhausting and emotionally draining. You must also be aware that a person who has been diagnosed with an eating disorder and who has accepted treatment can relapse at any time and withdraw from all treatment. Some people who relapse will re-enter treatment and others not. If your loved one relapses and then wants to re-enter treatment, they will need your love and support again to get through. Don't lose hope if your loved one relapses, and never give up hope on someone who refuses treatment. There is always hope, and someone who is willing to re-enter treatment is being humble and admitting defeat. Give them another (and maybe another and another) chance at recovery. Many people do find recovery after a good few attempts. The hold of eating disorders and the process of wrongful thinking can be very compelling and difficult to break.

These on some tips that will help you cope and accept life with someone who has an eating disorder:

• Accept the situation: don't try to over-analyze or rationalize anything, it is what it is

• Take everything day by day: don't focus too far ahead and don't backtrack in time

• Don't allow your life to revolve around the eating disorder: live parallel to your loved one, but don't allow yourself to become consumed

• Educate yourself as much as you can on the specific eating disorder your loved one has

• Join a support group or get therapy so that you can express your thoughts and emotions freely without worrying about the impact they will have on anyone else

• If something happens that makes you feel helpless, accept the feeling because you are helpless over the eating disorder

- Allow yourself a regular time out; take a holiday, go to the movies, get out and do something that excludes your loved one and the situation

- Maintain a normal family life: don't withdraw from other family members

- If possible, keep close family members involved in a supportive way

- Don't attempt to police your loved one; it will never work, and all relationships have to have a measure of trust

Working Through your Guilt

After the initial shock of the diagnosis that your loved one is suffering from a potentially life-threatening eating disorder, you can easily be overwhelmed by guilt. You could feel responsible for not realizing that there was a serious problem sooner, or you could berate yourself for accepting the lies and excuses you were fed. All of these feelings are normal, but they must not become the norm.

At the core of your guilt could be that you failed to live up to your expectations, your attachments, of what a good parent, child partner should be and do. And maybe you did ignore red flags? Your guilt will also be rooted in the sense of responsibility that you have to your loved one. But eating disorders are cunning and secretive diseases of the mind, and most sufferers go out of their way to be deceptive about their obsession. Don't carry your guilt for too long!

Guilt is a major negative and unnecessary emotion in people who are supporting someone with an eating disorder. If guilt is clouding your vision of reality, it is important that you eliminate it as quickly as you can. Guilt is a wasted emotion that can only hold you back. If you want to support your loved one through the painful process of recovery from an eating disorder you will have to adopt the role of witness and bastion; you cannot afford to be weighed down by guilt.

If you cannot shed your guilt, it is best to go for counseling, even if just for a short while, to help you move on. Here are some questions that you can ask yourself every time guilt raises its head in your mind. Keep them close by and answer them over and over until guilt stops plaguing you:

- Why do I feel guilty?
- What factor is at the core of my guilt?
- Does my guilt change anything?
- Does my guilt make sense?
- Does my guilt halt progress?
- How does my guilt affect other people?
- Should I be feeling guilty?

Once you have come to grips with your guilt, it is important that you take steps to protect yourself from future guilt. When you love someone who has an eating disorder, it is very easy to fall back into guilt. You could also be on the receiving end of accusations for your loved one or other people who are close to both of you.

Here are some ways to avoid feeling guilty:

• Avoid indulging in self-blame: the more you blame yourself, the more you open yourself up to blame from others

• Don't allow others (including your loved one) to blame or criticize you constantly: the more you allow, the more they will find wrong with you are your actions

• Rid yourself of unrealistic expectations and overly high standards

• Live according to your standards, not those of others: stand firm for what you want and what you believe in

• Don't use guilt on others: the guilt will rebound back to you because you are trying to control what you are not in control of

• Don't over-promise or over-commit: when you are in a stressful situation you need time, and if you don't keep your promises and commitments you will end up feeling guilty

• Don't make major changes in your life when you are under pressure: hasty or poorly planned decisions can cause more problems in your life and leave you with guilt and regrets

Guided Virtual Reality Meditation

I'm recommending guided virtual reality meditation to help you cope with the shock of learning that your loved one has an eating disorder. Having your worst fears confirmed can be extremely stressful, and can leave you feeling overwhelmed. You most probably still have other responsibilities that you have to take care of every day over and above. Why virtual reality meditation? Because it allows you to disconnect from your reality for as long as you can afford, without you having to leave home. The human mind can easily go out of kilter when it is overstressed, and virtual reality meditation allows you to switch off and rebalance your mind.

Traditional meditation would be excellent at this stage because it is proven to rebalance a stressed and confused mind, but if you are not already practiced in traditional meditation, you will probably not be able to relax sufficiently at this time to find real value. Guided virtual reality meditation is not true meditation, but it is a wonderful way to unplug and relax your mind.

All you need is a virtual reality headset and a mobile phone; it's that simple. You can then download any number of virtual reality meditation apps. Choose guided meditation apps where you will be guided through various types of meditation. You can also choose to have the meditations with or without music. The meditation destinations are endless! You can choose from ocean scenes to snow-covered mountain tops, and everywhere in-between.

Virtual reality takes you right to your destination. It is as if you are right there. You can see every angle and image, and you live the experience without having to leave home. Virtual reality meditation relaxes you by distracting your mind from its immediate reality, and most often our immediate reality is the catalyst of our stress and anxiety. As your mind learns to relax and you learn to let go, you will be less inclined to want to control everything around you.

Chapter 5

Debunking Myths about Eating Disorders

Because eating disorders have only recently been brought to the public's attention as a serious mental illness that causes serious physiological conditions and potentially death, little is known about the condition and myths abound. So does shame and secrecy!

Just because the public has only come face to face with eating disorders in the last few decades does not mean that people did not suffer from eating disorders previously. In the past (and even today) the condition was swept under the carpet, or people put up with it without understanding what they were facing. Under these circumstances recovery is not possible, so many people with eating disorders died from their condition, but their death was attributed to something else. And it still happens today.

Myths understate the condition and trivialize the desperation of the sufferer. Many myths are conveyed with sarcasm, so adding humiliation to the suffers' plight. All myths are ignorance and stubbornness on the part of those who perpetrate them; they refuse to open their minds. In cases where myths are perpetuated because of shame, those who perpetuate the myth place their ego before the wellbeing of a family member or loved one.

These are some of the common myths that abound about eating disorders:

1.   *Eating disorders are a lifestyle choice motivated by vanity.*

The most common myth was covered earlier on in this book. Nothing could be further from the truth. Although bodyweight does become an obsession with everyone caught in the grips of an eating disorder, it has very little, if anything to do with vanity. Most people who get caught up in obsessive, self-destructive behaviors have low self-esteem. Eating disorders develop over a long time, and no one chooses to develop an eating disorder.

2.   *Parents are the cause of eating disorders.*

Parents are crucial to recovery, but they are definitely not the cause of eating disorders. There is no evidence that upbringing makes a significant contribution to developing an eating disorder. While upbringing can be directly linked to low self-esteem in many cases, not everyone with low self-esteem develops an eating disorder. The statistics prove this, with millions of people around the world walking around with low self-esteem, but a very low percentage of them have an eating disorder. Even in families where eating disorders are commonplace, not every family member is affected. Science assumes that there is a genetic link, and research is ongoing.

Parents and family can play a crucial role in recovering from eating disorders. Where family support is absent, recovery is difficult and in many cases unsuccessful. Families also carry the burden of an eating disorder together with the sufferer. The disease has far-reaching consequences and often leaves everyone feeling powerless and helpless.

3. Eating disorders are a phase or attention-seeking.

Many people believe that eating orders are a 'phase' of bad behavior and attention-seeking, or an attempt to punish the family. This is completely untrue! No one chooses to develop an eating disorder, and most sufferers do their utmost to hide their condition from their family. Many will put up with severe physical illness and pain, but keep it from their parents and family. If it does come out that they have an eating disorder, most sufferers feel a deep sense of shame and guilt because of what they are bringing on their family. To add to the situation, many sufferers contend with ignorance and rejection from their families.

4.   *Eating disorders are not serious; people outgrow them.*

Unfortunately not! Eating disorders are a very serious condition and must not be ignored. Apart from the fact that they are life-threatening, they also invite other complications like substance abuse and depression. You cannot outgrow eating disorders, but you can be taught how to control them by professionals who understand the condition.

5.   *Eating disorders are the domain of affluent suburbs and white girls.*

Eating disorders are not selective about who they choose. Anyone is vulnerable to developing an eating disorder. The causes are as yet mostly unknown, but professionals and treatment centers list their patients as people of all ages and from all walks of life. Eating disorders have nothing to do with wealth or food at all. They are a mental illness that happens to focus on food and eating, but amongst many other things too.

6.   *Only girls, women and gay men develop eating disorders.*

This myth borders on the bizarre and is a typical denial of a patriarchal society. No one is immune, and that includes men and boys. In recent years some high profile sports stars and athletes have spoken out about their battles with eating disorders, including men. Hopefully more high profile men will speak out to debunk this sexist myth for once and all.

7.   *Someone who has a normal body weight cannot have an eating disorder.*

People with binge eating disorder, bulimia nervosa or unspecified eating disorders don't have to have excessive weight loss or weight gain. Eating disorders are a behavioral obsession that has changes in weight as a symptom. Eating disorders are a disease of the mind that have physical and medical complications and consequences.

8.   *Treatment and weight gain cure eating disorders.*

Eating disorders are never cured! But they can go into remission. With the rights tools learned in therapy, and enough love and support, a suffer can maintain control over an eating disorder. Unfortunately, if the suffer does not maintain a strict recovery program, they will relapse. Also, despite every effort, a suffer can relapse if faced with severe emotional stress or pain. Once you have developed an eating disorder, you have to maintain your recovery daily. Recovery must become a part of daily life, and you can never assume that you can relax your recovery program.

9.   *Once a person starts eating normally, they are cured.*

As with the point above, an eating disorder is never cured, it goes into remission. Eating normally and gaining weight is a positive sign that recovery efforts are going well. The focus of all treatment around eating disorders is on suffers' mental state of mind and mental wellbeing. Early treatment focused on physical health and possibly food, but ongoing treatment is on mental health.

Chapter 6

Treatment of Eating Disorders

Once your loved one has been diagnosed with an eating disorder, it is vital that treatment commences as soon as possible. If there is any delay in treatment, your loved one could change their mind and decide that they don't want treatments. For someone suffering from an eating disorder, the thought of treatment is very frightening. The fear of the unknown is just as frightening because most people suffer from an eating disorder for some years at least before they surrender to their problem and accept treatment.

It is at this time in particular that you must show your loved one support. Anyone in early treatment and recovery is very vulnerable, and the pressure around the situation can cause them to withdraw from treatment and relapse. Tell your loved one that they have your support and follow up your words with positive actions, like regularly visiting if they are in a hospital or a treatment center. If your loved one is getting outpatient treatment, spend as much time with them as you can. Go shopping together, go to the movies or take up a hobby together. Anything that will allow you to spend time together without focusing on the problem.

Surrender and Acceptance

Surrender and acceptance are vital to recovery from any traumatic experience that must be healed. Without surrender, the sufferer will hold on to reservations that they can control their problem, or believe that they cannot live without their problem. That can sound odd, but many people come to define themselves by problems or traumatic situations. They have made a life for themselves in which the problem is key to who they are and how they live. If someone has done that, letting go of the problem becomes very difficult because it requires that they redefine their life and who they are.

Surrender is unlikely unless the person has suffered the dire consequences of their eating disorder, and without surrender, there cannot be acceptance.

Depending on how long your loved one has been caught in the clutches of an eating disorder, they may or may not be willing to surrender. There is no way that you can know if they are willing, because you never know what someone else is thinking, and people often say something contrary to what they are thinking. Some people will go into recovery and accept treatment with the intention to fool everyone into thinking they are genuine while they

87

continue with their self-destructive obsession in secret. Other people will start treatment and then walk out. If the does happen, you must accept that your loved one is not ready to surrender yet and there is little that you can do at this point.

Trying to force someone into surrender is not going to work in the long run. They might appear to give in to your demands, but what will most likely happen is that resent will build up, and they will become even more secretive about their self-destructive eating disorder. If your loved one is an adult, they could choose to move away from you, or avoid you. Eating disorders are deep-rooted and have a very powerful hold over the sufferer's mind, and they are very deceptive so your loved one can believe that they can control their problem without treatment and without you.

If that does happen, it is time for you to back off! Give your loved one some space to calm down and get themselves back together. When you do speak again, tell them that you accept their decision to leave treatment and that you are always there for them irrespective. Don't speak about treatment, but keep on showing your love and support. Wait to see if your loved one broached the subject of treatment again. If they do, encourage them without putting pressure on them. If they don't, you can start raising the subject gently and gauge their response. If the response if vehemently negative, back off again and try again in a few weeks.

Some people will respond to gentle and supportive grooming. By grooming your loved one to accept treatment, you are appealing to their common sense and digging through the illusion created by the eating disorder. To do that there must be a strong bond of trust between you and your loved one. If your loved one surrenders and accepts treatment after you have groomed them, you must maintain the bond of trust and support that has been developed.

Acceptance follows surrender. Once your loved one has surrendered to the fact that they have an eating disorder that they are powerless over and that they need professional treatment to recover, they will begin to accept the gravity of their problem. Acceptance is a very slow progress that gains momentum as recovery progresses. No one needs to accept the whole problem at first; all that is necessary to go into recovery is to accept that there is a problem.

There is little value in trying to comprehend the whole problem in early recovery because eating disorders are so complex and deep-rooted. It takes years to come to grips with the reality of eating disorders, so don't waste time and precious energy trying to figure it out. Take it one step at a time, day by day. Don't go back in time and don't go forward in time. Keep yourself, and your loved one anchored in the present only, and appreciate every step forward.

Professional Treatment

Once your loved one has been diagnosed with an eating disorder, medical treatment will most likely be the most pressing issue. Extensive blood and physical tests and examinations will diagnose physical conditions that must be treated. These can range from vitamin and mineral deficiencies that can be easily treated, to ongoing and lifelong treatments for conditions like kidney failure or heart disease.

Medical treatment is condition-specific, and generally, there are a number of conditions that must be treated simultaneously. In most cases, medical treatment will be ongoing for months until your loved one has reached optimum health again. All medical treatment is initiated by potent doses of vital vitamins and minerals to promote physical healing and boost appetite. In instances where the physiological damage has been extensive, the condition might not be cured but rather contained or controlled. In those cases, medical treatment will be an ongoing lifelong process, but for many anorexics, their body restores itself to full health after a period of medication and proper eating.

A dietician could also be brought in because when most people with eating disorders enter recovery, they have become almost totally alienated from food. Their relationship with food and eating has become totally distorted. Apart from providing balanced daily meal plans that will aid in healing and recovery, a dietician can also help someone recovering from an eating disorder to re-orientate themselves psychologically with food and eating. When working together with a physician and a psychologist, a dietician can help someone recovering from an eating disorder overcome food issues identified through medical treatment and psychotherapy. In early recovery, many sufferers struggle with the taste, smell, and texture of foods, and that can genuinely bring on nausea and loss of appetite. A good dietician that understands eating disorders can teach someone in recovery how to enjoy eating food again, and it almost always doesn't take long to rediscover the pleasure of food and eating properly.

Continued, sound psychological treatment is essential to recovery. Unfortunately, this is the part that most people suffering from an eating disorder want to avoid in early recovery because exploring painful memories and emotions hurts. The fear of exposing emotions and pain that your loved one has gone to great lengths to avoid takes courage, and you must support your loved one through therapy. It will not always be easy for you because you will most likely be worn out yourself, but having non-judgemental love and support is key to long-term recovery.

What to Expect from Psychotherapy

During psychotherapy, your loved one might become distant and not want to discuss issues with you. As hurtful as this might be, you must accept the process if you are confident with the skills of the therapist. A person in recovery has a long road to travel, and it is a lonely one that often requires solitude and introspection. The therapist will at some point suggest journaling, which is a solitary process of writing down your own thoughts, emotions and maybe even creating a storyboard of their life. This is a very personal experience; resist the temptation to pry or read anything, even if your loved one is a minor because that will create trust issues that could lead to relapse. They also have to learn to accept their own emotions and learn how to deal with them. Emotional pain is another major issue that must be addressed, exposed, accepted and resolved. This is all a big ask for a vulnerable person who is most likely not in the best of physical health either.

When you do start speaking about therapy your loved one could begin by lashing out in anger. Accept the anger without needing to become defensive, but don't ever allow yourself to be abused verbally or otherwise. If you do have any blame to carry, acknowledge it, explain yourself, apologize and then move on. It has to pass and cannot become an obsession with either or both of you. Joint therapy sessions are excellent for working through issues that make you feel guilty, and your loved one feel done down or angry. Most therapists and treatment centers encourage and welcome joint and family therapy sessions. The point and purpose of recovery are to understand and accept past events, to learn how to cope with similar situations in the future. Acceptance should be followed by forgiveness, and then everyone should be able to move on. No one is intended to become stuck in the therapy stage.

Where therapy is successful, you will find that your loved one will become psychologically stronger, and then have an innate need to tell and share with someone. All humans have a need to share traumatic experiences with at least one other person to free themselves from the emotional pain. That is when you will be most needed, and when you will have to stay patient and strong to get your loved one over the last hurdles to begin healing. You will need to be a witness to your loved one's story and pain. No matter how difficult you find it, you will need to hear your loved one out if you want them to heal and if you want the person they were before to return. Many events will most likely be repeated over and over again. Some events could be totally alien to you, or downright horrific. Listen without judgment. Be patient and listen without interjecting, and even without comment if necessary. Often a brutalized soul doesn't need words; they just need a loving presence and nothing more.

Therapy can include some or only one of the following, as well as therapies not mentioned:

- Behavioral therapy
- Cognitive analytic therapy
- Cognitive-behavioral therapy
- Focal psychodynamic therapy
- Interpersonal psychotherapy
- Family intervention
- Family group therapy
- Ego-orientated therapy
- Occupational therapy

Remember, someone with an eating disorder's mind has become overridden by wrongful thinking patterns. Medical treatments and psychotherapy are tools in the arsenal of a willing sufferer that they will use to rewrite their thinking and maintain ongoing recovery.

Complementary Therapies

Recommending complementary therapies is becoming more frequent as their success is recorded and proven for treating people with eating disorders. Complementary must not, however, be viewed as a replacement for medical and psychological therapies. They should be included with medical and psychological therapy to enhance the quality of life of your loved one.

There are many different complementary therapies available, so that will allow your loved one o choose an option that appeals to them.

Complementary therapies include:

• *Dance Movement Therapy:*

It allows people to explore alternative ways of coping as well as expressing emotion. It is also a form of artistic expression that can serve as an outlet for unexpressed emotions. Therapists observe and evaluate movement, and suggest interventions as required.

• *Art Therapy:*

Art is used as a medium of communication and expression. Through creativity, people are encouraged to express their personal experiences and stories under the guidance of a professional art therapist using clay, drawing, painting, and sculpting.

• *Animal therapy:*

Animal therapy is used to develop emotional growth. Dogs and equines are the most regularly used animals. The

94

premise is that emotional bonds develop between people and animals and that bond fosters emotional healing. Many studies have revealed that caring for an animal can be an empowering experience, and basic care, grooming and taking an animal for walks can increase self-esteem. All animals used are trained therapy animals, and the process is undertaken with the guidance of a therapist.

- *Acupuncture:*

Acupuncture is derived from Traditional Chinese Medicine and dates back thousands of years. Fine needles are painlessly inserted into acupuncture points along the body to treat specific physical, psychological and emotional conditions.

- *Kinesiology:*

Kinesiology suggests that the human body has an innate healing energy that flows it. It proposes that sometimes this energy needs to be readjusted because it can become blocked. Through working on physical and emotional stressors that block energy, a kinesiologist can rebalance the body and clear blockages. Areas targeted include nutrition, emotions, physical pain and mental issues.

- *Meditation:*

Meditation is an ancient spiritual practice that has been proven to be beneficial for the treatment of anxiety, addictive behaviors and pain management. Meditation is also known to realign thought patterns and promote self-acceptance. Over a period of time, mediation can reverse obsessive behaviors and self-destructive coping mechanisms.

- ***Yoga:***

Yoga promotes self-care and mindfulness. It is proven to reduce stress levels and encourage clear thinking, which in turn can lead to improved mental and physical health. Regular practice encourages people to become re-attuned with their bodies and stay grounded. For someone suffering from an eating disorder, yoga can improve their attitude and relationship with food as something that feeds their body and promote health and wellbeing.

- ***Mindfulness:***

Mindfulness teaches people to respond to their thoughts without judgment. It teaches acceptance and compassion and being present in the moment with your thoughts, feelings, and emotions and with your body. Everything as it is at the moment. Mindfulness teaches people recovering from eating disorders to deal with shame and guilt.

- ***Virtual reality meditation:***

Virtual reality meditation is not really meditation, but rather o form of relaxation. Its use by medical practitioners and psychologists is growing rapidly as it does relieve tension. It is proving very helpful for patients who are awaiting a painful procedure like dentistry or an operation. They are given a post-operation session of virtual reality meditation to relax, and it is proving to be very successful. It relaxes by distracting the mind from its immediate reality. As the mind relaxes, it lets go of fear and anxiety.

Chapter 8

When Recovery Doesn't Happen

As your loved one progresses in treatment and you become more accustomed to the fact that your loved one has an eating disorder, you will most likely start wondering where this will lead. Don't think too far ahead because there is no definite outcome. Recovery is possible, and it is the outcome that everyone wants, so keep your hope and focus on recovery.

Unfortunately, there are also other outcomes that you must keep in mind, but not focus on. Eating disorders do come with a high suicide rate, and suffers can die from medical complications of the disease.

Although your ongoing love and support are crucial to your loved one's recovery, you have no control over the recovery process. Only your loved one has control over their own recovery. And there could be instances where your loved one does want to recover, but there was too much physiological damage already done before they went into recovery, and that costs them their life.

If your loved one does not manage to go into successful recovery, or if they commit suicide, or if they die from complications of eating disorders you will quite rightly feel devastated and be wracked with guilt. Although that is a normal reaction, you must seek professional counseling and support. You must accept that whatever the outcome, you did your best and recovery was never in your hands. This is where the three C's come into play.

What are the 3 C's

The 3 C's form the core to understanding your role in eating disorders.

The 3 C's are:

You did not Cause your loved one's predicament; sustaining an eating disorder is a choice.

You cannot Cure your loved one's disease; choosing recovery is their choice.

You cannot Control your loved one's disease and its symptoms; it is always their choice.

The majority of people who love someone who has an eating disorder are deeply affected by their loved one's mental illness. Their emotions are constantly in upheaval, leaving them feeling helpless, powerless, profoundly sad, fearful, angry, betrayed and with many more negative emotions that dominate their everyday. Don't feel guilty if you feel like that; it is a normal reaction.

Unfortunately, eating disorders can have a very powerful hold over the sufferer, and only they can opt to seek treatment. Their brain has fallen into a pattern of wrongful thinking that they have come to believe and you have to accept that. Your loved one is out of touch with reality!

Sometimes people with an eating disorder will lay blame on family and loved ones to elicit guilt and deflect attention from themselves. Take responsibility if there is truth in any accusation, but don't take responsibility for the perpetuation of the eating disorder because of what you may or may not have done, particularly if your loved one is refusing treatment. Blame is an excuse to deflect personal responsibility and avoid professional treatment and intervention

Your loved one might try to manipulate you into trying to get their own way, particularly if they have a problem with binge eating. Stand by what you know and stand your ground. Don't get involved in an argument because an argument centered around is manipulation is an argument without rules. Rather leave the conversation than give in because you cannot cure their situation.

However your loved one chooses to manage their eating disorder, particularly one professional help and intervention has been offered and is available is their choice, not yours. You did not cause their problems; you cannot cure their disease Only they can, and you cannot control their behavior or the outcome and consequences of their actions.

Remember too that if your loved one is of legal age, as an adult, they are free to live as they please. You cannot, and have no right to dictate your lifestyle preferences to another adult. But you do have the right to tell them that their lifestyle is unacceptable to you and unless they are willing to seek professional help and treatment, you no longer want anything further to do with them. You can add that if they are willing to seek professional help and treatment, they will have your absolute support.

Accepting this can be a long process and a bitterly painful experience. Your loved one has a mental illness that has transformed their thinking and negatively affected their health. The person you loved and knew can only come back if they are willing to undergo ongoing treatment to restore their physical and mental health, and rewrite their wrongful thought patterns to return them to sanity.

That decision lies wholly and completely in the hands of your loved one!

Suicide

Anorexia Nervosa has the highest rate of suicide among people suffering from eating disorders, followed by bulimia nervosa and binge eating disorder. Suicide is more prevalent in people who have a substance abuse problem or suffer from chronic depression or other mood-related disorders together with an eating disorder. Anorexics tend to plan suicide for some time before making an attempt on their own life, whereas, in people suffering from other eating disorders, suicide attempts tend to be more impulsive.

Society holds a common perception that suicide is a cowardly act. Nothing could be further from the truth! The only skill we are born with is the instinctive skill to survive. There are countless reports of children and adults surmounting impossible odds by doing things way beyond their normal capabilities to survive in life-threatening situations.

Suicide then goes completely against the only instinctive skill we have! To fly in the face of our survival instinct does not only take courage, but it also takes the direst form of desperation! A desperation that completely overwhelms our survival instinct and equips us with the courage to take our own life. Suicide is when the problems we are faced with appear to us to be so extreme and dire that we can see no way out. We conclude that death is the only way we can escape this burden and desperation gives us the courage to take our own life.

Suicide in itself is difficult to understand, so too put it in context with eating disorders makes it even more complex. Prevalent conditions that can contribute to suicide include:

• They believe that they are not good enough

• They believe that they can never find recovery

• They set unrealistic goals for themselves and strive for perfection, and repeated failure leads to increased feelings of worthlessness

- They develop a profoundly distorted sense of reality

- They are malnourished, and that affects their thinking

- They feel that they are a burden to others and others would be better off without them

Because eating disorders are a very secretive disease and the suffer agonizes through it alone and in secret, eating disorders are often accompanied by thoughts of suicide and suicide attempts. There are always warning signs before any suicide, and people with eating disorders often give subtle clues of their intention to commit suicide. These include:

- Speaking about being in intolerable pain and feeling trapped

- Speaking of wanting to, or being ready to, die

- Speaking of having nothing left to live for

- Speaking of being a burden to others, or holding them back

- Preoccupation with death

- Increased substance abuse

- Heightened anxiety, agitation or reckless behavior

- Anger and rage

- Extreme mood swings

- Oversleeping or insomnia

- Withdrawing from people and loss of interest in life

- Putting personal affairs in order
- Giving away previously prized possessions
- Calling or visiting people to say farewell
- Suddenly appearing happy or at peace

Processing Premature Death

Educating yourself on the realities of loving someone who has an eating disorder right from when the diagnosis is first confirmed will open your eyes to the reality of their problem, the dangers of the lifestyle that they have chosen and prepare you for the fact that they might not recover successfully.

You have to accept that there was nothing that you could have done to prevent the death, and there is nothing that you did that caused the death. Guilt is the ever-present wretched companion of people who love who had an eating order that has died. Guilt is a pointless and wasted emotion that will negatively impact your life if you do not find a means to rid yourself of it and come to terms with the reality that you were powerless over the situation that played itself out at the time of your loved one's death.

Once the initial shock abates and you are left with the profound sorrow and grief, as with any death you must seek additional emotional support to help you through the process. Grieving the death of someone who had an eating disorder comes with the additional pain of guilt, self-blame, questioning yourself, your right to have been a parent, a child, a partner or spouse. Although normal, you must have professional support to process these thoughts and emotions and then detach yourself from them. You do not deserve to suffer for the rest of your life because your loved someone who rejected recovery. It is not your burden to bear!

Find a grief counselor, therapist who deals with eating disorders, or group therapy sessions for support from people who can identify with your pain. Also, seek spiritual support through whichever religion or spiritual belief you hold. It is vital that you get support from people who understand and know that whatever your loved one did or became, you will always love them and you have every right to love them.

Broader society can be very judgemental, and the death of someone who was diagnosed with a mental illness is often met with cold callousness. Don't let that attitude touch you; you loved someone who had an eating disorder, and genuine love never dies. Also, don't carry any shame that society may place upon you. You need never be ashamed of your deceased loved one, and you need never be ashamed that you love someone who died of an eating disorder. Lying to society to keep face means lying to yourself, and lying to your-self will invite depression and other emotional ills into your life. You owe society nothing, and anyone who judges you or your departed loved one is not worth knowing!

Chapter 9

Is there Life after Eating Disorders?

You want to know if recovery from an eating disorder is possible. Unfortunately, the answer is yes and no; some people do well in recovery, and others don't do well and relapse. Eating disorders are never completely healed; they never go away. It is rather like cancer that goes into remission. When cancer is in remission, it can return at any time and so can eating disorders.

It does not matter how long a sufferer has been in recovery, relapse is only a hairsbreadth away at any time. That is something that you must accept, and that your loved one must not only accept but must believe. Your loved one must keep to a strict recovery program that they will be taught at a treatment center, or by a psychologist. And they will need your love and support always.

Relapse

Relapse is a reality, and most people will relapse at least once but mostly a few times before they come to grips with recovery. While relapse might seem devastating to you and your loved one, in reality, it is part of the learning curve. As long as your loved one admits to relapse, treatment can continue. If the relapse was brief, there should not be any serious medical complications.

If your loved one hid a relapse for an extended period, there could be medical complications that will have to be treated, but the psychological impact is far more severe. Anyone who hides a relapse while perpetuating their self-destructive behavior has reservations about recovery. In other words, they are not mentally prepared for recovery, and therefore not committed to their recovery. This calls for serious psychological therapy to uncover the reason for the reservations. Only your loved one can expose the reason for their reservations.

For many people who have been in recovery and relapse, relapse is a great teacher. It takes the person right back into the heart of their mental illness and the insanity that prevails in that state of mind. People find this space both frightening and abhorrent, and it quickly gets them to admit to the relapse and back into their recovery program. If that happens, you can be assured that there has been progress in the recovery process; your loved one is starting to see their problem from a rational perspective.

Relapse is not always a bad thing as long as it is picked up quickly, your loved one takes responsibility, and the reasons behind it are addressed.

Apart from reservations, there are other triggers for relapse, the most important of which are external stressors that trigger anxiety. This is particularly true if the person has not yet developed sound coping skills. Issues like relationship problems, job loss, financial stress and death of someone close are often the main triggers for relapse.

Successful Recovery

As mentioned previously, total recovery will never happen. Anyone with an eating disorder will stay in recovery until the end of their life. Ongoing recovery is only maintained through vigilance and keeping to a strict recovery program every day. There can never be any days off, and it is best that the recovery program is incorporated into everyday life. People who do well in recovery tend to expand their daily recovery efforts rather than slacking off. This is done by wilfully introducing daily routines that work with recovery and good health and wellbeing. Recovery is something that must be nurtured and fed to keep it going. People work towards recovery; recovery does not work for them. Recovery must be viewed as an ongoing activity.

Recovery is also about developing an attitude of hope and working on developing spirituality. In recovery, people have to believe that they are not alone, and this goes beyond human relationships. A strong spiritual foundation must be cultivated. Having faith that there is a loving power greater than ourselves, who has our best interests at heart gives a person the opportunity to let go of having to control everything. Being able to let go of all concerns and burdens and hand them over to a higher power is of great consolation to someone suffering from an eating disorder.

In early recovery, the problems can seem so overwhelming that many people feel that they cannot see a way out. Having faith that you can release your burdens to a higher power is what strengthens many people, and helps them to keep moving forward. Almost everyone who is successful in recovery has a very strong spiritual foundation that they maintain daily.

Personal commitment and dedication, professional help, the love and support of loved ones and a strong spiritual connection are what make ongoing recovery possible.

A Bit of my Backstory

I have been in recovery from eating disorders for almost a decade, and for two decades from substance abuse. My problem was eating disorders from a young age, but I picked up substance abuse problems for a while as well, as a way of medication the mental and emotional pain that were a constant in my life. I would like to give you some insight into my mind when I was caught up in the grips of anorexia nervosa and bulimia nervosa so that you can try to comprehend the insanity.

But before I try to give you an idea of what goes on in someone with an eating disorder's mind I want to briefly visit my attitude towards food and eating in childhood. I must mention that I had never heard of eating disorders until years after I was caught up in them, and no one in my family knew anything about eating disorders either. Also, no one close to me dieted regularly or had any issues with food, so there was no mental preconditioning. But I had issues with food for as far back as I can remember.

My earliest memories of eating and food were that I did not eat much and I did not eat regularly as my brothers and cousins did. When food was served, I often ran away. When I did eat, I was a fussy eater. Food had to look a certain way and be prepared in a certain way otherwise I wouldn't eat it. A few examples (and there are many) was that I would not eat cereal, but I would eat cooked porridge on condition that it was burnt; if it was not burnt, I wouldn't eat it. I would only eat bread with the crusts cut off and only if it was cut into small triangles. I would only drink tea from a cup that was filled to the brim and spilled when I picked it up. I refused to eat meat, chicken or fish; I did not like the smell and texture. I picked at food and smelt it before I ate it. If it did not look or smell right, I wouldn't eat it. I carved my food into tiny pieces and ate very slowly. I threw food from my plate onto the floor. Sometimes I insisted on eating with a small teaspoon, so eating took even longer. I sneaked food (particularly meat and fish) into a napkin and gave it to my brothers after meals. Obviously, I was a small thin child.

People told my parents that I am spoilt and they must leave me and I will eventually eat. They tried that, and I didn't eat. A doctor told them to feed me outside of regular mealtimes if I asked for food and that did work. I also ate fruit and vegetables very easily, but obviously, my parents knew that that could not sustain me. But I was not an unhealthy child.

When I was in grade two, a teacher asked my mother if she was aware that I gave my lunch box to other children every day. Needless to say, my mother was horrified. She took the time to pack me healthy lunches, and she believed that I was eating them. Once I started school, I refused breakfast, so that is why my lunchboxes were well stocked. I insisted that the lunchboxes stop. As I got older, I started refusing to eat when I came home from school too, and gradually worked my way to eating one meal a day in the evenings. No one could force me to eat; I refused to eat.

By my mid-teens, I had developed anorexia nervosa without knowing what it was. A few years later I had added bulimia nervosa to my woes. Many people would ask how no one noticed, but I know that I went out of my way to hide what I was doing from my mother (by that time a young widow because my father had passed away very unexpectedly at a young age). I was willfully deceptive while my mother trusted me. I blatantly lied to my mother to protect my self-destructive behavior.

Back to my mind to give you an idea of what goes on in the mind of someone who has an eating disorder. What went on in my mind will be along a similar line as for other people who have eating disorders. The exact thought content will differ, but the insanity and destructive power of those thoughts will concur.

So here goes: in the very early days I knew very little about calories or kilojoules, so I set up an amount of food that I would allow myself in one day (in pieces and teaspoons). I would very closely monitor my food intake, and if I ate more than I had allowed myself in one day, I had to pay a penalty the following day. That was the basis of my disease for twenty years. It was an insane secret system of minimal self-reward and maximum self-punishment.

Somewhere along the way I found out about kilojoules (in my case) and adopted a daily kilojoule count for someone on a strict weight loss diet. I was aware that such a low daily kilojoule count must not be maintained for an extended period, but that did not worry me. For the rest of my time as an anorexic and occasional bulimic, I planned my daily food intake according to an extremely low kilojoule intake. At the end of the day, I would calculate how many kilojoules I had eaten, and if I had eaten more than I should have, that amount had to be deducted from my kilojoule allowance the following day. I also reduced the next day's kilojoule allowance by 10% because I had overeaten. The same rule applied for the following day, and the next and the next. I had to pay penalties for going over the number of kilojoules I had set. Sometimes a penalty was to fast the next day. Then I could only drink tea because my eating was out of control according to me.

The burning hunger pangs that woke me up in the middle of the night were a victory cry for me; I had conquered my desire to eat!

Bulimia nervosa would step in along the line, but I was only bulimic in times of severe emotional distress. Bulimia nervosa was not as complicated for me: the little I had eaten should not have been eaten, so I got rid of it within minutes of eating by vomiting. Bulimia nervosa was very straightforward for me.

There were times when I did not have bulimia nervosa at all, and the anorexia nervosa was toned down considerably. These were always happy times, and times when I could cope with what was happening in my life.

But anorexia nervosa would always come back, and bulimia nervosa popped in to visit now and then.

I was well aware of the dire state of my health, but nothing stopped me.

Eventually, my mother found out (by this time I'd long since left home, got married, got divorced, got married again and got divorced again). The situation was awful, but I just couldn't carry on living like I was, and I did the thing that I had always worked so hard to avoid; I told my mother, the only person that I really trusted. I know that she was devastated and that she could not understand how it happened and why I did to myself what I did. She blamed herself and tried to find answers in the past. I know that I caused my mother a lot of pain. I know she cried bitterly.

But then my mother bounced back! I was in outpatient treatment, and she surprised me by telling me all about anorexia nervosa and why people get it. She had accepted it, wanted to do something positive about it and wanted to help me recover. That was the greatest gift anyone has ever given me in my life.

We both had our own lives, and we lived apart, but my mother not only supported my recovery, but she also showed her support constantly. She accepted the diagnosis, she accepted the situation, and she gave me her unconditional love and support with empathy. My mother was a non-judgemental witness to my story. She asked questions and told me when she didn't understand, but she never condemned me. That is what someone who is trying to recover from an eating disorder needs.

My mother and I had always been very close, but we became even closer in my recovery. My mother is the only person, apart from professional counselors, that I have opened up to about the nightmare of anorexia nervosa, bulimia nervosa, and substance abuse. My mother will always be the only person that I will ever need to witness that hell. Recovery requires only one person to support you genuinely. She was willing to walk through that pain with me, and that was enough for recovery and healing. We discussed relapse and triggers. I was able to be very open in the comfort of the trust I had in my mother and the faith she had in me. But there was one thing we never discussed. What would happen if she was no longer there? Now, in retrospect, I think that she was too scared to raise it with me because I know now that she did mention it to other people.

That reality came in August 2017 when my mother passed away very suddenly and unexpectedly. It was the greatest test of my recovery. There could be no greater test for me because my mother was always the pillar of my recovery, no matter where either of us was or how much distance separated us, I could always reach oy to her, and she was there.

It has been difficult without her. At first, it went reasonably well, but December caught me unawares. She loved the mid-summer festive season, and it is also her birthday month. Grief overcame me throughout December and well into January. And then I woke up feeling good again and life went on. I fled to Google: "am I normal?" Google told me "Yes!" The loss of a close loved one can be profound and almost debilitating for six months and longer. Grief is worst on special occasions. I'm normal!

I have faced the greatest challenge to my recovery and remained normal. I did not fall back on any self-destructive coping mechanisms. My coping skills are good. I have felt the emotional pain and loss and walked through it as well as other people do. My mother and I faced the unspoken fear we both held, and I came through it. I am still in recovery!

So to answer the question "is recovery from eating disorders possible?" Yes, it is!

I owe my recovery to my willingness to surrender when I just could not carry on anymore. Also to the professionals who embraced me with kindness and taught me the skills I lacked, to other people who had suffered as I had, and who opened their hearts to me, to my mother who accepted what she could not understand to support me, and to the grace of a loving God.

And the next question you probably have "do you recover completely, and live as if the eating disorders never existed?"

No, I am still not a big eater, but I do stick rigidly to three meals a day. I do that not because I am hungry (often I'm not), but for my physical health. There are still times when eating is a real drag for me, but I take note of my thoughts and then push through whatever I'm eating.

I am vegan for many years. Apparently, that is a symptom. I don't know. I became vegan because I could not accept the taking of a life for something as trivial as a meal. I still

115

feel that way. It was something that was discussed extensively in therapy and with the physician that was treating me. The consensus was that I have a right to my beliefs and as long as I eat a healthy, balanced diet there is no problem. There are no vegetarians or vegans in my family, nor have there ever been that I know of. I am still a happy, healthy vegan.

I am still an overachiever, and that has led me to be a very successful businesswoman and entrepreneur. Were my high standards and desire to succeed a symptom? I don't know.

There are a few other symptoms that could apply to me, but not many. All I know is that I had issues with food from my first memories. From early childhood, I wanted to do well at everything I took on; I worked hard to achieve. I was an anxious child, and I still am an anxious woman. I spontaneously clench my jaw and my fists regularly every day. I've done it all my life, and I have no idea why I do it.

Very shortly into treatment, I decided that I would not try to find out why I had developed eating disorders, but rather focus on what they are and how to cope with the condition. I look at it as someone who is diagnosed with cancer. Whether it is genetic, lifestyle or unknown makes no difference to the fact that they have got cancer. They have to undergo treatment, and hopefully, their cancer will go into remission.

I look at recovery from eating disorders in the same way. Why I developed eating disorders is not the prime factor. I use and build on all the tools that I have been given in recovery. Things, like being vigilant of my thoughts, acknowledging negative thoughts, but not reacting to them and staying away from things that can potentially set me off again like weighing myself or counting kilojoules, are part of my daily life. So is meditation, spirituality, and faith. These things keep me strong.

Recovery is definitely possible, but all the work and effort must come from the person suffering from an eating disorder.

One last thing!

I want to give you a **one-in-two-hundred chance** to win a **$200.00 Amazon Gift card** as a thank-you for reading this book.

All I ask is that you give me some feedback, so I can improve this or my next book :)

Your opinion is *super valuable* to me. It will only take a minute of your time to let me know what you like and what you didn't like about this book. The hardest part is deciding how to spend the two hundred dollars! Just follow this link.

http://reviewers.win/eatingdisorder

Where to find more Information and Support

Most people have no idea what to do when faced with a loved one who is trapped in the clutches of an eating disorder. There is still a lot of ignorance and myth surrounding eating disorders and many people's response is "just get over yourself!"

People suffering from eating disorders cannot "just get over themselves". They are caught up in mental illness, and they need medical and professional help to get them onto the path of recovery. Unfortunately choosing recovery is your loved one's choice, not yours.

For the loved ones of someone who is suffering from an eating disorder finding valuable information can be like trying to find a needle in a haystack! You need to be educated about the challenges that you are facing. Information on eating disorders is becoming more readily available as science and medicine make the broader public more aware. Rehabilitation and treatment centers for eating disorders are gaining popularity, but most treatment is still on an outpatient basis.

There are some very informative websites and books available that will help you understand eating disorders.

Recommended Books:

The Treatment of Eating Disorders

Carlos M. Grilo

James E. Michell

Eminently practical and authoritative, this comprehensive clinical handbook brings together leading international experts on eating disorders to describe the most effective treatments and how to implement them. Coverage encompasses psychosocial, family-based, medical, and nutritional therapies for anorexia nervosa, bulimia nervosa, binge-eating disorder, and other eating disorders and disturbances. Especially noteworthy are "mini-manuals" that present the nuts and bolts of 11 of the treatment approaches, complete with reproducible handouts and forms. The volume also provides an overview of assessment, treatment planning, and medical management issues. Special topics include psychiatric comorbidities, involuntary treatment, support for caregivers, childhood eating disorders, and new directions in treatment research and evaluation.

The Encyclopaedia of Feeding and Eating Disorders

Tracey Wade

The field of feeding and eating disorders represents one of the most challenging areas in mental health, covering childhood, adolescent and adult manifestations of the disorders and requiring expertise in both the physical and psychological issues that can cause, maintain, and exacerbate these disorders. The scope of the book is an overview of all the feeding and eating disorders from "bench to bedside", incorporating recent changes introduced into the Diagnostic and Statistical Manual of Mental Disorders, Fifth Edition (DSM-5). The aim is to present one of the first complete overviews of the newly defined area of feeding and eating disorders with respect to genetics, biology, and neuroscience through to theory and its application in developing clinical approaches to the prevention and treatment of feeding and eating disorders.

Websites:

National Eating Disorder Collaboration

http://www.nedc.com.au

National eating Disorder Association

https://www.nationaleatingdisorders.org

Behind the successful front, survivor of drug addiction, alcoholism, self-destructive behavior, toxic relationships, domestic violence, depression and more as I tried desperately to find society's acceptance and approval.

Through total surrender – a point where I genuinely begged the God I had always refused to recognize for help; a dim light of hope appeared. Unable to carry on living as I was any longer I actively sought help and found it. I began to find healing.

Once you find self-love and self-acceptance, no judgment or retribution can touch you; you find the freedom to be yourself. Once you accept the presence of an ever-present, ever-loving spiritual power that is much greater than you, you can relax, stop trying to control everything and finally live. The dim light of hope becomes ever brighter until it completely embraces you and eventually begins to radiate from you. Let go and let God!

-   ***Biella Blom***

Printed in Great Britain
by Amazon

29082461R00070